ACROSS THE KALAPANI

The Bihari Presence in Mauritius

edited by
Marina Carter

CRIOS
CENTRE FOR RESEARCH ON
INDIAN OCEAN SOCIETIES

Cover Design and Illustrations:
Neermala Luckeenarain, 1999

Layout:
Prospero Books

Photographs:
Mahendra Koreemun and Siven Kaullee

© **Marina Carter, 2000**

Published by:
Centre for Research on Indian Ocean Societies
 PO Box 138, Port Louis
London Office: 92 Greenfield Road, London N15 5ER

Printed and Bound in Great Britain

ISBN 99903-52-03-8

Contents

	Page
Preface	
Introduction	9
Bihar: The Migratory State *M. Carter & S. Deerpalsingh*	15
North Indian Slaves and Settlers in Dutch and French Mauritius *Marina Carter*	25
Bihari Convicts in Mauritius *Clare Anderson*	35
The Characteristics of Bihari Recruits *Saloni Deerpalsingh*	43
The Journey of Bihari Indentured Labourers *V. Govinden*	57
Life under Indenture: Bihari Migrants' Stories *Marina Carter*	67
The Recreation of Tradition: Marriage and the Family under Indenture *M. Carter & V. Govinden*	87
The Making of a New Community: Socio-Economic Change and the Bihari Hindus *M. Carter, S. Deerpalsingh & V. Govinden*	101
Socio-Economic Mobility among Bihari Muslims *Amenah Jahangeer-Chojoo*	119
Religious and Cultural Traditions of Biharis in Mauritius *Sarita Boodhoo*	133
Conclusion	151
Notes on Contributors	153

Preface

This book is the first of a new series to appear under the auspices of the Centre for Research on Indian Ocean Societies (CRIOS), an NGO created in 1997 by a group of social scientists based in Mauritius.

To date the centre has published a trilogy of books dealing with Mauritian history which aimed to retell the story of settlement from the foundations of French colonial society to the present: through stories of co-operation and cohabitation which created the foundations of creoledom in *Colouring the Rainbow*, through an assessment of the hidden histories of labour immigrants in *Forging the Rainbow*, and by the articulation of modern voices in *Consolidating the Rainbow*. A fourth book, *Stepping Stone of Immigrants*, which sought to recreate the historical heart of Mauritian society, through a depiction of the old Immigration Depot or Aapravasi Ghat site in the island's capital, was published in 1998.

CRIOS has now decided to mark this dawn of the new Millennium, and the four centuries of human settlement of Mauritius, with a celebration of the diverse and successive waves of people whose million-strong descendants currently call this small volcanic outcrop in the Indian Ocean home. The *Presence* series traces the immigration and settlement of the groups which have emerged to claim a distinct ethnic heritage in the modern era, and assesses the cultural continuities and compromises which characterise them.

We begin this new series with an in-depth analysis of the origins and evolution of the Biharis of Mauritius. Following a two hundred year cycle of ethnic regroupment and fracturing on the island, creating a present-day situation in which numerical imbalances are checked by in-group divisiveness, the Biharis remain the linch-pin of the Mauritian polity. Every Prime Minister since Independence has been recruited from the ethnic group whose descendants arrived from this state. The Biharis in Mauritius today do not form a cohesive unit, spread as they are into various religious groups, with differing levels of attachment to their ancestral origins, but the numerical preponderance of immigrants from this populous Indian state ensures that their descendants will continue to play an important part in the life of the island.

Acknowledgements

I would like to thank the following:

all the contributors who worked against tight deadlines to bring this book to fruition

James Ng Foong Kwong for help with the conceptualisation and realisation of this book

Avinash Ramtohul for his assistance with computer graphics

Neermala Luckeenarain who deserves special thanks for once again providing the evocative illustrations used in the book

Khal Torabully and Abhimanyu Unnuth for allowing us to feature their graphic and vivid poems

The staff of the Mauritius Archives and the Mahatma Gandhi Institute where much of the research for this book was conducted

Barbara Grunwell of Prospero Books for her skills, advice and support

Tom Carter and Donna Giang in the Cayman Islands for allowing me the use of their computer and fax

The friends and family of myself and fellow CRIOS members in Mauritius and England.

Marina Carter
January 2000

Introduction

Whilst CRIOS research has until now focussed on the ways in which traditions of cultural syncretism and newer expressions of ethnic identity have transformed and fragmented the 'communities' settled in Mauritius, the *Presence* series traces the evolution of each of the regional, linguistic or religious threads which today make up Mauritian society. The purpose of this series, far from harking back to the filio-pietism of earlier community-based studies, is to unearth the archive-based roots of immigration and to chart the evolution of the descendants of each group as its members have surmounted the early difficulties of settlement, integrated in the host society and embraced available opportunities. Above all, the series seeks to unravel the distortions and myths which have accompanied the search for ethnic identity and political recognition in modern Mauritius. 'Invented tradition' is very much a feature of this complex nation and it is the purpose of this and forthcoming *Presence* volumes to understand and explain the mechanisms by which self-constituted groups demarcate themselves and compete for resources within the nation state. The 'distinctiveness' which is claimed by the several 'communities' recognised customarily and constitutionally in Mauritius may be real to us all, but like any social construct is based on a mass of compromises which the tools of historical and sociological analysis readily unveil. To be a Bihari, or a person of Bihari descent, may seem a simple concept, free from confusion or distortion. Yet the state of Bihar itself has undergone modifications, whilst the absorption of other minority ethnic groups into the present-day self-defined community of Biharis has been a continuous feature of Mauritian social evolution.

The first contribution to this volume delineates the changing shape of Bihar and introduces the reader to the location and economic history of this populous state situated in the 'bhojpuri belt' of India. Bihar, with its hill-dwelling tribals and troublesome dacoits was viewed with trepidation and curiosity by the British and has never quite lost its dubious reputation as a backward and lawless region. At the same time, Bihar is still in many respects the key to understanding the average Indian. It is the pulse of India - the concerns of the Hindi heartland beat across the country.

Because much of Bihar was subsumed within the larger state of Bengal well into the 19th century, and regional origins were poorly recorded, it is difficult to trace pre-indenture Indian settlers in Mauritius to a specifically Bihari origin. Nevertheless the presence of Dutch and French settlers in Bengal and the evidence of slave trading and free migration of Indians from this region of north-eastern India, points to the likelihood of a sprinkling of Biharis accompanying the slaves and settlers generally known as 'Bengalis' into Dutch Mauritius and the Isle of France. This is reinforced by the discovery of Indian slaves given a surname, 'Patna', which refers to a district in Bihar where the French possessed a 'loge' and from which they may well have originated.

Clare Anderson's work on the convicts who were sent to Mauritius before the abolition of slavery and prior to the mass arrival of Indian labourers under the indenture system, provides the first irrefutable evidence of the arrival of Biharis on the island. Her contribution gives us a glimpse of the presence of the Bihari 'dacoit' and rebel in early British Mauritius. As Dr Anderson points out, the convicts, though small in number, were a highly visible community in a largely creole society. The extensive records kept by the British about the convicts, also provide details of the caste status of the all male Bihari convict group.

Saloni Deerpalsingh's contribution follows up on this study of the smaller group of Bihari convicts by providing detailed information of the caste status and regional origins of the much larger Bihari population who arrived in Mauritius from 1834 as indentured plantation labourers. Their categorisation and classification by the British and Indian officials who supervised their shipment and allocation to estates has left a written record of caste or religious affiliation and regional origin which is invaluable as a guide to their many descendants who continue to identify with such labels to determine group membership and even choice of marriage partners. The continuity of caste demarcations over the century and a half which has elapsed since indentured migrants first arrived is particularly remarkable. Age and marital status was also recorded, whilst the language spoken by most of the Bihari immigrants - Bhojpuri - can be inferred from regional data.

The journey of migrant labour was not simply the physical trudge to the emigration depot in Calcutta and the long sea voyage to Mauritius - it also represents a period of transition. This is highlighted by V. Govinden who outlines the role of indenture as an intermediary and crucial form of semi-bonded labour which straddled the uneasy years between the abolition of slavery and the modernisation of the plantation sector in Mauritius. For the individual migrants, also, the journey overseas entailed a momentous time of change, an embarkation to a new life, and one from which the majority would not return. If, in the early years, Biharis were not always aware of the distance they were travelling, or the duration and terms of their indenture contracts, over time migration to Mauritius became an established feature of life in some areas as villagers returned to collect families and to recruit other labourers. Whilst indentured migration has sometimes been depicted as the last resort of the desperate, V. Govinden shows that selection procedures at the emigration depot meant that only the young and healthy were recruited, although increasing family migration allowed a relaxation of rules to enable the very elderly to accompany their relatives to Mauritius. The traumas of what was for many their first sea voyage, and the dangers of the months' long passage by sailing ship are vividly described. The comradeship which developed between fellow travellers, however, gave Bihari migrants a lasting source of strength and brotherhood, known as *jehaji bhai*, which sustained them through their indentureships.

The themes of recruitment and the voyage are picked up again in the next chapter which uses the medium of migrant's own stories, through statements and depositions made by returning labourers, to recount the first hand experiences of participants in the indenture system. The migrants tell of their working lives in Mauritius and provide assessments and insights which are absent from most official accounts of indenture. Hostility to plantation discipline and rules, the petty harrassments of old immigrants and, above all, the dignity and stoicism of those Bihari pioneers shine through their stories. Boodhoo Khan, the sepoy who became a sirdar and was subsequently sent home in disgrace, encapsulates the life experiences which preceded and surrounded indenture, and epitomises the stalwart and proud bearing of migrants, again in sharp contrast to the frequent depiction of them as victims in the history books.

The traditional appraisal of indentured labourers as single male migrants, exiled from family in solitary camps overseas, is also contested in the succeeding contribution which details the regroupment of families in the Mauritian setting. The early years of the migration which saw a massive disparity between numbers of men and women arriving, was corrected by the mid 19th century, through a combination of imperial directives, financial incentives, and migrants' own actions in sending for and collecting their families in India. A kind of marriage migration also took place, with male Biharis already settled in Mauritius competing for the arriving single women at the depot. Family life and the marital relationship underwent stress during the indenture system, as the low levels of civil marriage and birth declarations complicated inheritance rights and traditional power structures. The young age at which children could be indentured and condemned to the juvenile reformatory also diminished the parental rights of immigrants. As Biharis moved off the plantations and into settlements which were to become new villages in Mauritius, they were able to recreate customary means of celebrating marriages and resolving conjugal and family disputes.

The re-establishment of Biharis in village settlements is followed up in the next chapter which deals with avenues of economic mobility and the redrawing of the religious and cultural map of Mauritius. Those indentured labourers who rose out of the ranks of field workers to become sirdars and job contractors, led the way in seizing opportunities offered by the dismantling of the larger sugar estates to establish themselves as landowners, small planters and entrepreneurs. Large landowners were instrumental in funding and supporting projects to recreate the sacred topography of India with the construction of temples. The creation of spokesmen and leaders for this new community was not without difficulties. Contesting claims are typified in the disputes that arose at the turn of this century connected with the organisation of the Maha Shivaratree festival. On a more local level, however, the dependence of the immigrants on unsatisfactory state mechanisms of redress was lessened by the re-establishment in the villages of panchayatis and baitkas. These village institutions became the core of the new communities of Biharis which established themselves all over the island. The baitkas and other village meeting places of Biharis also provided the bases from which the sons and grandsons of sirdars and other immigrants were to launch themselves into the political arena over the coming decades.

Dr Jahangeer-Chojoo's article continues the theme of socio-economic progress of the Biharis by providing a detailed account of the avenues to mobility presented to Muslims settled in Mauritius. Using case studies of remarkable families, she demonstrates the ways in which Bihari Muslims used land acquisition and parcelling, trading, and other activities to enhance their prestige and status within the community. The Bihari Muslims have incorporated minorities from the south and west of India and together they are designated as 'Calcuttyas' to differentiate them from those Muslims, principally Gujaratis, who came to Mauritius not as indentured labourers but as free traders. Dr Jahangeer-Chojoo also assesses the links between these two groups. As with the Hindus, those members of the community who had advanced economically, sought to consolidate their position by taking a leading and benevolent role in the establishment of mosques and *madrasas* or religious schools on the island.

Finally, Sarita Boodhoo takes us on an exhaustive and enchanting journey into the cultural world of Biharis in Mauritius. She demonstrates the inter-connectedness between the bhojpuri language which the immigrants brought, and the creole from which they borrowed and which they influenced. Bihari dishes and their use on the island are detailed, as are the plethora of rites, rituals, festivities and traditions which have survived, some in a more modified form than others, into the present day.

Across the Kalapani is a feast of Bihari culture, art, history and poetry. The legacy of Bihar to Mauritius lives on in the language and song, dress, and food of the island's population. This volume is an attempt to contribute to this rich and enduring legacy by highlighting the historical background and patterns of settlement of Biharis in Mauritius.

Bihar: The Migratory State

M. Carter & S. Deerpalsingh

Where do the majority of North Indians settled in Mauritius come from? During the British Raj their historical homeland, known today as the state of Bihar, was one of the four sub-provinces which formed part of the undivided Presidency of Bengal before 1911. The remaining three were Bengal proper, Orissa, and Chota Nagpur. Bihar achieved its statehood in 1936. It was separated from Bengal in 1911 and Orissa in 1936.

Topographically, Bihar occupies the northwest corner of Bengal and is bounded on the north by Nepal, on the west by the United Provinces of Agra and Oudh, by Chota Nagpur plateau and Burdwan division on the south and Raj Shahi division on the east. The broad Ganges river divides Bihar into North and South.

Colonial Policies and Resistance in 19th Century Bihar

Many Biharis were seriously affected by the range of policies adopted in the late 18th and early 19th centuries aimed at settling the countryside in the wake of the colonial conquest. The new revenue systems, law courts, and western legal concepts in the administration of land rights had little relevance to a society where hunting and gathering, pastoral and other shifting forms of agricultural economy were still important. The effect of introducing these measures in India was the destruction of the economic systems of rural communities such as tribals almost overnight. Sometimes this was done deliberately – by encouraging settled systems of agriculture the British hoped they could more easily be taxed. Whole communities were turned into migrants, sometimes almost overnight, forced to roam the countryside in search of work. The newly-established tea plantations in Assam, the coal mines, jute mills and steel factories of Bengal, and the more far off destinations such as the sugar plantations of Jamaica, Mauritius and Fiji were the beneficiaries.

In Chotanagpur and the Santhal parganas as a whole, 44 per cent of the population was still classed as 'tribal' in 1881, but the northern districts of Palamau, Hazaribagh and Manbhum had been extensively settled by Hindu immigrants even before the grant of the Diwani to the British in 1765. Here, up to 90 per cent of the population was Hindu by the second half of the nineteenth century, compared with only 10-30 per cent in the south. Increased pressure on the land reduced the most marginalised to the status of *kamiya*, or bonded labourers. By the end of the 19th century, the average size of holdings had fallen so low that peasant farmers could scarcely feed themselves: 'the great body of raiyats cannot indulge in what will be called a luxury in this country of a full diet of cereals all-round the years, as one contemporary wrote.

The Bihari poor did not accept their immiseration under colonial rule quietly. Those who retained some land and some independence usually put up the stiffest resistance, and thus during the Santhal *hool* or insurrection in Bihar in 1855, fighting continued for many months and some 10,000 were killed in British reprisals before the movement was effectively suppressed: a fateful struggle which turned the Santhal districts into one of the biggest sources of migrant labour in the second half of the 19th century. Large numbers of 'adivasis' and other labouring groups associated with early indentured migration were also involved in fighting during the great uprising of 1857, known as the 'Indian Mutiny'. There were a succession of uprisings by the Mal Paharias of Bihar, and spectacular insurrections staged by the Hos of Singhbum, and the Khonds of Orissa.

The criminalization of certain segments of the Indian population gave the British a means of controlling turbulent populations in the more inaccessible or 'lawless' parts of the state. According to these laws (most infamously the Criminal Tribes Act of 1871), whole communities such

Bihar and Surrounding States in Northeastern India

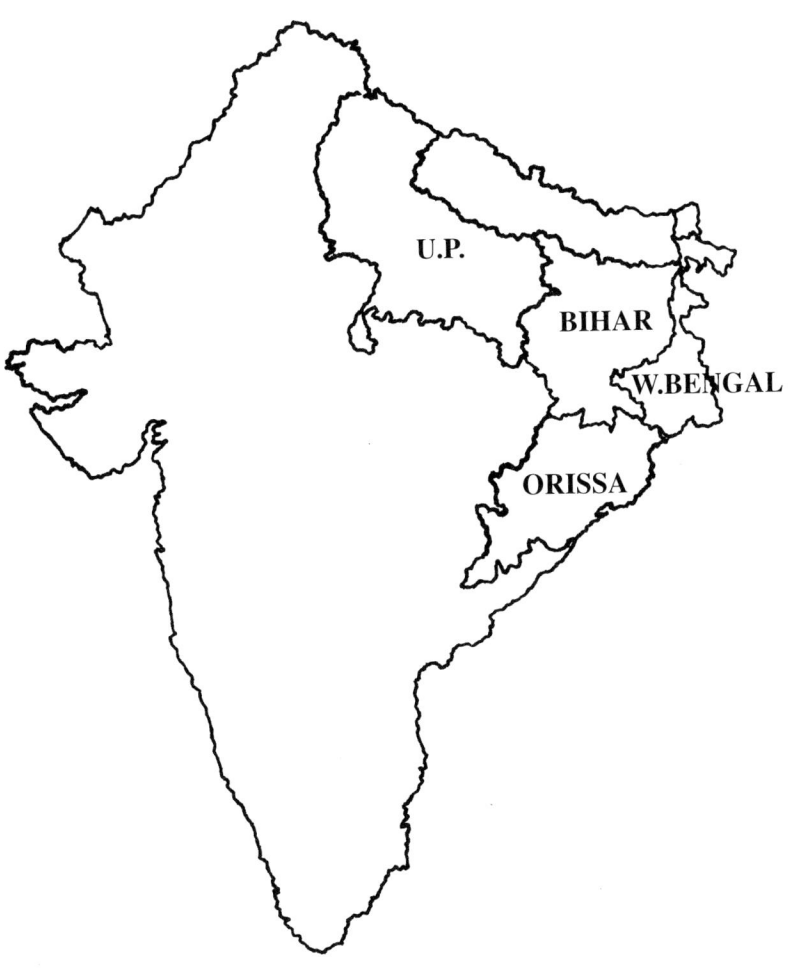

as the Maghyar Doms in Bihar were described as habitually criminal, and adult male members of such groups forced to report weekly to the local police.

Seasonal Migration of Biharis within Northern India

The Santhal insurrection produced a flood of migrants, mostly of Santhal, Oraon and Munda labourers into the north of Bengal, where they helped in the clearance of the jungle. From here they went on to the tea gardens in Jalpaiguri and Darjeeling. Famines, forest enclosures and population growth continually added to the ranks of migrants in the 19th century.

The steady intensification of cultivation which increased pressure on land and food resources, when combined with other characteristics of the economy such as the insecurity of tenures, population pressure and the extortionate levels of rent, meant that high rates of out-migration were inevitable from other districts of Bihar also. These factors added to the unreliability of harvests, together with the presence of recruiters in a particular district, and the numbers of returnees, all contributed to determine the degree of emigration from the various *thanas*, or subdivisions.

Under-employment in rural areas was the commonest cause of seasonal migration. Labourers would work in cities for part of the year and return home to cultivate their crops. Bengal was one of the most densely populated provinces in India, and the large jute-collecting centres like Narayangang, Chandpore and Serajganj, all employed large numbers of Biharis in reaping the crop. In Saran district in Bihar alone, between 80,000 and 200,000 of the total population were engaged in 'seasonal' migration. A typical seasonal migrant in the late 19th century was Hira, a Teli who lived in the village of Usri in Saran with his wife and two children. Hira farmed a small plot of land of less than two *bighas* and, unable to live on his earnings from this alone, was obliged to work for four months of the year as a porter or labourer in Calcutta.

Districts of Bihar

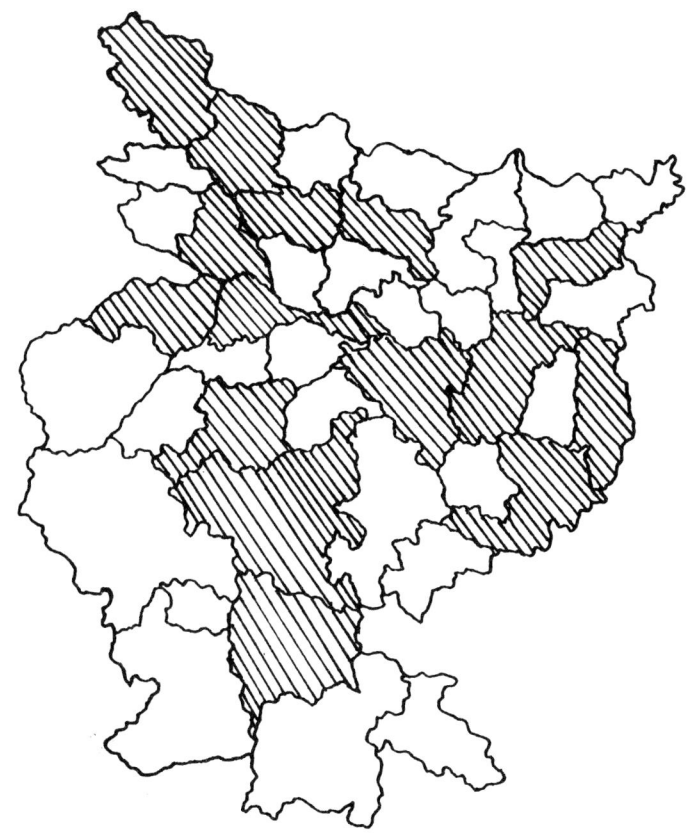

Shaded regions indicate districts which contributed a high proportion of recruits for Mauritius, namely Patna, Saran, Sahibganj, Gaya, Ranchi, Hazaribag, Purnia, Munger, Bhagalpur, Santhal Pargana, Bhojpur, Muzaffarpur, Darbhanga, and Champaran.

From Seasonal to Overseas Migration

A process of proletarianisation was therefore already underway when Calcutta - the port of embarkation and recruitment area for Mauritius - attracted those Biharis who were working far from home. In fact it was the presence of so many Bihari seasonal migrants which first drew the attention of labour recruiters working for the overseas colonies. They noted that a 'superabundance of labour' existed in Bengal which prompted hill coolies to "wander in search of work not only over all the Bengal provinces, but as far to the northwards as Delhi".

The tribal inhabitants of Chota Nagpur were among the first groups to be tapped as a potential work-force for indigo and tea production in early nineteenth century India. Indigo planters and businessmen such as Dwarkanath Tagore testified to the 'habitual migratory patterns' of tribals who were employed in manufacturing concerns in the 1830s. In seeking an appropriate labour force, Mauritian planters drew upon these experiences of capitalists operating within the sub-continent The contemporary appraisal of the Bihari tribal migrant is evident from this report, dated 1838:

> *'dangas ... entertain no prejudices of caste or religion, and are willing to turn their hands to any labour whatever ... In their own country they have but little rice, and eat snakes, lizards, rats, mice, etc. Their clothing is simple, and scanty and they eat only once, rarely twice, in 24 hours.*

As recruitment expanded, all Biharis from rural areas were welcomed by the Mauritian authorities who required that: 'especial Care be now taken to ensure that the persons who may be engaged shall have been known as really Agricultural Labourers in their own Country'.

In 1856 Mauritian planters, seeking new reserves of labour, informed Indian officials that the Santhals and other Biharis were 'labouring now under extreme destitution' and that migration could relieve them of the moneylenders 'who have driven them to rebellion and their present abject state of misery'. By this time, however, inhabitants of the Santhals in Bihar were less willing to migrate overseas, as opportunities developed within India itself. The Commissioner of the Santhal Parganas explained:

It is hopeless at present to expect Santhals to go to the Mauritius. They are far too well off and too fond of their own country. Here and there some scarcity is existing, but the rail, the coal mines, and the timber forest afford work for those fit for it, ... it is a great mistake to suppose the Santhals are in a state of abject misery.

Where better employments existed closer to home, long distance migration was shunned. The impetus of recruitment to colonies like Mauritius was only maintained, therefore, where villagers and families had developed ties overseas. What had begun as an exile rooted in desperation had become something akin to a chain migration, as more and more of the recruiting of Biharis was conducted by ex-migrants, and where a high proportion of arrivals consisted of individuals from the same villages and of family members coming to rejoin loved ones.

To suggest that Bihari migrants were little more than forced labour hustled unwillingly from their homes is therefore misleading. Migration became a simple means of betterment and of escape from the social and economic oppression of rural life, much of it imposed politically.

Bihar into the modern era

As Bihari migrants in Mauritius emerged from indentured servitude, parts of their homeland remained entrenched in the vicious cycle of poverty well into the 20th century. According to one survey, conducted in Sadr subdivision of Ranchi district in 1911, less than 20 per cent of the holdings amounted to 14 acres or more and could thus support an average family.

Long after slavery had been abolished in Mauritius, and even when indentured workers had mostly liberated themselves from the shackles of the sugar estates there, forms of bonded labour lived on in Bihar, under the term 'kamiya'. Debts incurred by impoverished families would force them to sell out their labour and even those of their children for decades ahead. The annual migration of some 250,000 Biharis from the east of India to the Punjab in the west, where they are employed as low-paid agricultural labourers at harvest time is evidence of continuing forms of semi-bonded migration, because the cost of transporting them, or their wage, has generally been paid in advance, often in a manner (such as in clearance of a debt) from which the labourers themselves are unlikely to benefit. Destruction of forests in the *adivasi* areas continued, with a million Biharis migrating into and settling in Chotanagpur in central India, for example, between 1951 and 1971.

The early established reputations of the rebellious Santhals and Kols, and the lurid accounts of *dacoity* and *thuggee*, even human sacrifice by tribals, tagged Bihar with the label of a backward and lawless region, for long after those events. With all its problems, however, and notwithstanding a sometimes undeserved notoriety, the state of Bihar is a key region in democratic Indian politics, and the views of its humblest inhabitants continue to make themselves felt in the subcontinent as a whole, just as they do today in Mauritius.

Sources and Guide for Further Reading

Historical works detailing the economic history of the region include S.C. Bose, *Peasant Labour and Colonial Capital*, 1993, and D.Rothermund, *The Indian Economy under British Rule*, 1983. For a good account of migration within India, see C. Schwerin's article in D. Rothermund and Wadhwa (eds) *Zamindars, Mines and Peasants* (1978).

Who said people ajar? People from Bihar!
We know the seven lotus circles of the oceans,
the parrots of Basauli fretting on the bar.
They called us friendly aliens,
natives of migrations from sugar to zukar!

Khal Torabully

A. Yang's *The Limited Raj* is a useful account of the background to migration at the district level. See C. Bates & M. Carter 'Tribal migration in India and beyond' in Prakash (ed) *The world of the Rural Labourer in Colonial India*, 1992, for a discussion of migration to Mauritius.

North Indian Slaves and Settlers in Dutch and French Mauritius

Marina Carter

It is notoriously difficult to determine with any degree of precision the region of origin and cultural background of slaves. Torn from their homelands and submerged into alien socio-economic systems where they were treated as chattels, records of slaves contain few clues as to their linguistic and cultural identity. It was important for slave-owners, however, to maintain control over their forced labourers by means of divide and rule. Ethnic diversity was one way of creating divisions and preventing the dangers of concerted opposition. For this reason, slave-owners adopted ethnic labels to identify and differentiate their workforce. The broad distinguishing terms they used provide the starting point for an assessment of the regional background of Indian slaves in Mauritius.

Slaves from Bengal in Dutch Mauritius

Dutch trade at the Indian ports and with other European nations plying the lucrative routes to the Indies and to the Spice Islands in the 17th century, inevitably produced an exchange of slaves along with other goods. Bengal was one of the earliest sites settled by Europeans in Northern India, attracted by the region's cotton, silk, sugar and saltpetre as well as rice production. The Dutch set up a base first at Hughli, and then at Chinsura in 1653, the French established themselves at Chandernagore in 1688, and the Danes settled in Serampore in 1755. The first British factory was also around the Hughli in 1650-1. In 1690 a site near the village of Kalikata, (later Calcutta) became the centre of British commerce. The usual designation for natives from the entire region (including parts of present day Bihar, Orissa and surrounding states) was consequently that of Bengalis.

India was not, however, the main base of the Dutch in the Indian Ocean. They had a large settlement at Batavia, and another at the Cape of Good Hope. It was consequently from Batavia that the first labourers were sent when the Dutch established themselves on Mauritius in the early 17th century. To these convicts were added Malagasies obtained from slaving voyages organised to Madagascar by the Dutch governors. The origins of the Indian slaves also found on the island, are less clear, probably because they were brought in small numbers on ships engaged in the transport of other commodities. We learn of their presence from incidental references, usually when misdemeanours had occurred and punishments were recorded. The slaves were all given Christian names by the Dutch settlers, but a place-name was usually appended, identifying the region of origin of the slave. Thus, when runaways were captured and the details of their cases sent to the Cape authorities, we can identify their ethnic status from their names: we learn, for example, about Antoni of Coromandel who was sentenced to a severe whipping, and to prevent him disappearing again, was placed in chains and an iron crown fixed on his head. Another deserter, Antoni of Malabar, was condemned to be whipped and kept in chains for 10 years.

If the South Indian slaves did not seem to bear their servility with ease, the Bengali slaves were just as rebellious: despite their relatively small number they were involved in at least two of the more serious attacks against the Dutch in Mauritius. In 1695 fire destroyed the principal Dutch settlement at Fort Frederik Hendrik in the South Eastern bay of the island. It did not take long for the authorities to realise that this was a case of deliberate arson, and when the insurgents were caught, it became clear that the destruction was part of a plot to kill the Commandant of the settlement along with his garrison based in the fort, to be followed by attacks on the individual homesteads of the free Dutch settlers. The band of conspirators was composed of four or five individuals: Aaron of Amboina had run away from the fort some months prior to the incident and was joined by Esperance, a Bengali woman slave, who ran away to be with her lover in the forests. Her friend Anna, also a Bengali slave, and two others, Paul of Ceylon and Antoni of Malabar, were recruited as accomplices. Around the middle of June 1695, Aaron and Esperance made their way back to the fort where Esperance roused her co-conspirators, and the group set fire to the complex of thatched wooden buildings. Within days the perpetrators had been caught and made to confess. Antoni and Aaron were sentenced to a horrible death: their flesh torn from their bodies by red hot pincers, while Esperance was strangled. Their bodies were hung from a gibbet. Anna and Paul escaped punishment through lack of evidence.

Fort Frederik Hendrik in Vieux Grand Port, Mauritius, before its destruction by fire.

In 1706 another Bengali, named Louis, was sentenced to a similarly tortured death for having plotted to kill the Dutch settlers. The series of revolts, and the torments inflicted on the Europeans by their runaway slaves, contributed to the decision made by the Dutch to abandon Mauritius in 1715.

Slave and Free Immigrants from 18th Century Bengal

Bengal continued to provide slaves to the French who took over the island in 1715. The main French settlement in Northern India was at Chandernagore in Bengal but the French were present in Bihar itself, with 'loges' at Patna and Chapra and lands in their environs. The slaves who arrived in the now renamed Isle of France were classified as Indians generally, or were assigned a broad regional appellation, identifying them as either Malabars or Bengalis. There is circumstantial evidence to suggest that some slaves were despatched from Bihar itself, but, in general, the identity of Bihari immigrants remained concealed behind their designation as Bengali throughout the 18th century.

There were Bengalis in the Isle of France from the early years of French settlement. In 1732 11 Muslim sailors including Ali Bengali, Secmouamod and Paquira were contracted to work on the island. The civil status registers also list the deaths of several 'topaz' soldiers described as natives of Bengal from the mid 1730s. By the mid 18th century, the presence of Bengali women slaves is indicated when the baptisms of their natural born children are recorded. Apart from the free Muslim sailors, these Bengali men and women are generally identified by Christian first names, such as Francisque and Sylvie.

Evidence of slaving voyages per se can be seen from entries in the registers dating from the 1770s when, conversely, unnamed Bengalis are listed as having died. The entry for 3 February 1770, for example, lists the death of a 'Bengali negress'. In 1772 it is evident that a cargo of slaves had recently arrived from Bengal, because the civil status register for Port Louis recorded on 3 July that "un noir de Bengale de la traite de Chandernagor" had died. Over the next few days, 5 more unnamed Bengali women from the same shipment were reported to have died. It is clear that very young Bengali children were being sold into servitude: in the same year a 7 year old Bengali child was baptised, as was a three year old Bengali boy who had arrived with his enslaved mother. Over the following years, scores of newborn children were born to Bengali slave mothers in the various districts of the island.

Some of these women were more the companions than the slaves of the men who owned them. The fortunate few were rewarded for their roles as companions and mistresses and were freed along with their children. Thus, a free community of Bengalis emerged in the Isle of France, becoming land and slave-owners in turn. Some of the Bengali women even married European men in the colony. In 1771 the marriage of the Breton Pierre Dufour with Marie Christine, a Bengali woman and his former slave, was celebrated in the district of Moka. Marie Christine's death was recorded at Port Louis in 1783, when she was 45 years old. During the years of the French Revolution, such marriages across the colour line became more common. In 1793 Gabriel Roilet from Chartres married Anne, the daughter of a Bengali woman.

Fewer in number, but important to the growth of the Bengali community, some male slaves were also enfranchised. Their numbers were supplemented by free Bengali men who arrived on the island – thus in 1809 the death of Pierre Louis Maga, a 40 year old fisherman born in Bengal, is recorded. Their marriages with women from the same region created the genesis of an identifiably Bengali segment of the free coloured community whose creole-born children also intermarried. Thus, as well as contributing to the foundations of creole society through their relationships with white Europeans and with other Asian or African immigrants, the Bengalis constituted an identifiable community into the 19th century.

The size and importance of the Bengali community is demonstrated by census data in which the place of birth of free property owners was recorded. In 1788 the ownership of lands and property of the coloured community was enumerated: numerous Bengali families were cited among them. Thus, Baille and Marie, his 40 year old wife from Chandernagore, owned 52 arpents of land, whilst Marie Manique of Bengal owned 156 arpents of land and possessed a total of 11 slaves. Veronique Guedon, also from Bengal, possessed a similar acreage of land and owned 14 slaves. In some cases, the date of arrival of individuals is given. Thus we learn that Lascard Sadoux, a Muslim born in Calcutta, arrived in 1766 aboard La Catherine. He was now a fisherman. The occupation of the 51 year old Bengali woman Demay Poline was that of cake maker. Flore Bazeilhac, a 29 year old Bengali woman who owned 150 arpents of land and 19 slaves, had arrived in 1771. By 1806 the Bengali free community was even more numerous. A list of households in the Eastern suburbs of Port Louis revealed that 122 were headed by Bengalis – almost equal in size to the South Indian population brought from the larger French comptoir of Pondicherry.

This community itself was composed of different strands. Both Muslims and Hindus arrived from Bengal during the period of French rule, and whilst many were given Christian names soon after arrival, as they acquired property and status in the Isle of France, they also exercised a choice of marriage partner based on their own religious affiliations. Mahmoud, described as a lascar fisherman born in Bengal, married in Port Louis in 1794. The witnesses at his wedding were all fellow Muslims, and despite his locally-born wife, also of Indian origin, bearing the Christian name, Marie, she may well have been a Muslim herself. The likelihood of Muslim women bearing Christian names is demonstrated by the record of another marriage between the 23 year old Bengali son of Rahim Khan and Canansa who married the Bengali girl, Rose. The bride was the widow of a man named Mohamed and her parents were also evidently Muslim, named Sheik Cocaille and Amboutie, respectively.

Whilst some region of origin data is available for the free Bengali community, most of the slaves' birthplaces are impossible to trace. However some data is available from records of the slaving voyages undertaken to source these forced labourers. In 1785 flooding and the failure of crops in East Bengal led to the sale of hundreds of children who were embarked on boats and taken to Calcutta. An enquiry was instituted to uncover the extent of the trade.

Other voyage accounts reveal that slaves exported from Bengal were exposed to disease and died in large numbers. Peter Horrowbow, commander of the 'Friendship' purchased 130 young people in Chandernagore intending to take them to Mauritius, but was obliged to turn back when 40 of the slaves died within a few days of embarkation. He diverted his course, and sold the slaves in Colombo.

By 1789, the Governor General of India, Lord Cornwallis, was decrying the "infamous traffic" carried on by "foreign European seafaring people and traders, in purchasing and collecting native children in a clandestine manner, and exporting them for sale to the French islands" and the slave trade was abolished from the British and French territories in Bengal that year. Clandestine shipments continued, nevertheless. When the Stisam Low was intercepted as it left Calcutta for Pondicherry, details of the slaves found on board were given. The 20 girls and 8 boys were mostly aged between 6 and 13. The oldest girl was only 17 years of age. Several had been kidnapped and passed from buyer to buyer. Mirham's case, was typical: stolen from the house of her parents by one Moondhee Mahjee, she was sold to a Mr Sampson and then on to Monsieur Jourdan, the supercargo of the vessel. Most of the children came from what is today West Bengal: Chinsurah, Chandernagore and Calcutta itself were the chief places of origin.

This was one of the few documents which revealed the actual districts of origin of the Bengali slaves. Furthermore, because slaves were usually given French Catholic names by their owners, their birth names are not mentioned in the available records. In a few cases, however, a Hindu or Muslim creed, or a place of origin, was appended to the name of a slave. Thus amongst the many slaves listed as 'bengali' in the first British slave registration of 1819 mention is made of a Charles Patna, who was a 32 year old cook in Port Louis, and of a Nancy Patna, a 30 year old laundress, also residing in the capital of Mauritius. Charles was the slave of Jacques Mallac, and was described as 5'2 tall and tattooed on his right arm. Nancy's owner was one Joseph Lautier, and she was 4'11 in height. The names are significant, because they represent one of the few indications of the presence of Biharis amongst the North Indian slave community on the island.

Pour mémoire, ma seule langouti, un pagne,
ma langue engloutie.
Si vous me reconnaissez, je vous prie,
appelez-moi esclave prête-nom,
homme de paille ou bouche-trou,
kapok des champs ou vertèbres d'océan.
Mais sachez que mon sabre de sang
m'a déraciné jusqu'à la moelle.

Khal Torabully

Shipments of North Indians to Mauritius, which began in the Dutch 17th century, and continued through the French 18th century, did not completely cease in the British 19th century, despite the ban on slave trading. British advances in the European fight for supremacy in India meant that the French had successively lost control of their Indian 'comptoirs' by 1810. They responded by moving their slave trading from Indian shores to the ships in which the British plied their commerce, and resorted to kidnapping the Indian crews. When the Treaty of 1814 restored to the French their 'loges' in Bengal, the British Governor General of India took the opportunity to demand that these new victims be freed. He reported that the individuals concerned "are stated to have been captured by the French in English vessels, in which they were acting either as lascars or menial servants" and addressed the Governor of Mauritius with the request that the freedom of these Indian slaves be purchased.

Robert Farquhar, the British Governor at Mauritius responded that great difficulties had been experienced in ascertaining the whereabouts of the captured and enslaved servants and sailors. He added, however, "while the sepoy force was maintained here, I was enabled by their means to ascertain some instances of this nature, which were instantly acted upon by me, and freedom restored to the parties".

Some of the Bengali slaves brought to Mauritius either during the 18th century when the trade was legal, or as a result of piracy at sea, and clandestine importation, went on to take up positions of some respectability in the British administration. In 1817 a pion named Boodhoo is recorded as having been allocated a female slave for his own use. These and numerous other individuals from the Bengal Presidency, including a few from Bihar itself, were to be of immense help to British officials when first convicts, and then indentured labourers, were brought to the island from the Indian subcontinent.

Sources and Guide for Further Reading

The archival material used in the preparation of this article is chiefly taken from the following sources: the T 71 series at the Public Record Office, London, the British Parliamentary Papers on the Slave Trade and the Civil Status records of the Archives Nationales d'Outre Mer, Aix-en-Provence, France. One of the most detailed of published accounts of slaves in the Dutch period remains K. Heeringa's 1895 study, *Les Neerlandais aux Iles Maurice et Madagascar*. M. Jumeer's 1984 thesis on the Indian population of the Isle of France entitled "Les Affranchis et les Indiens Libres a l'Ile de France au 18e Siecle" is likewise unsurpassed. I have also made use of my own article "Indian Slaves in Mauritius, 1729-1834" in *The Indian Historical Review*, vol xv.

Bihari Convicts in Mauritius

Clare Anderson

The history of Indian immigration to Mauritius has largely been written in terms of indentured labourers, shipped to the island to work on sugar plantations. However, another little known but important aspect of Mauritian history was the transportation of Indian convicts to the island during the early nineteenth century (1815-37). Though the numbers were limited – just 1500 convicts were sent – their demographic impact should not be underestimated. Almost 1000 arrived in 1815 and 1816 alone, at a time when the population of the island was largely composed of slaves and creoles. The first census in 1826 recorded a total population of just 86,000. Thus the convicts were a highly visible community.

The convict transportation system

Indian convict transportation was crucial to British attempts to consolidate control in the Indian Ocean. When Robert Townsend Farquhar arrived as the first British Governor of Mauritius, the slave trade had just been abolished. This had potentially serious consequences for the supply of labour. Any threat to the socio-economic supremacy of the Franco-Mauritian plantocracy ran the risk of causing serious anti-British unrest. The importation of convict labour was thus an attempt to guarantee stability. Farquhar initially colluded with the Franco-Mauritian planter class in illegal slave importations. In the long term, however, he can have been in no doubt of the need for a source of labour to replace slaves. It was in this context that he instigated the transportation system.

The convicts transported to Mauritius primarily worked on public works projects, clearing land, quarrying and building and repairing roads and bridges. They were a valuable labour force, vital for the development of the colonial economy. Indeed, when transportation to Mauritius was abolished in 1837, there were many complaints about the worsening condition of the roads. It has even been suggested that the presence of convict labour influenced the later decision to import indentured Indians to work on the plantations. The Commission of Enquiry, set up to examine labour conditions in 1875, reported that the fact that Indian convicts had already been imported made the Indian indentured labourer 'not the entire stranger he was in the West Indies and Demerara'.

The socio-economic origins of the Bihari convicts

Most convicts sent to Mauritius were transported from the Bengal Presidency, which at this time encompassed large regions of modern north India and Bangladesh. 104 of the convicts whose region of origin can be traced to Bihar (14.4%) came from the following districts: Bhagalpur, Patna, Purnea, Ramgarh, Saran, Shahabad and Tirhut. The Bihari convicts were all male, mostly *shudra* peasants: agricultural labourers or village servants, such as water-carriers or bearers. Caste groups included *goala* and *hajam*. The next largest category were Muslims. A significant proportion were tribal *(adivasi)* peoples, who lived separately from Muslims and caste Hindus. The smallest group were from the Brahmin, *kshatriya* (warrior) and merchant *(vaishya)* communities. They included a handful of *rajputs.*

The crimes for which the convicts were transported were diverse. Broadly speaking, they reflected the nature of transportable offences in the early nineteenth century. As such, they are similar to the crimes for which all convicts in the Bengal Presidency were transported to Mauritius. However, there is some divergence between the two groups. Convicts from Bihar were more likely to be transported for the serious offences of gang robbery or murder, as opposed to highway robbery. By far the largest proportion of the Bihar convicts - 45.2% - had been involved in *dacoity,* several in large gangs. Highway robbery and other larceny offences accounted for the next largest number of convicts (19.2%

and 12.5% respectively). A smaller number were transported for burglary and other offences including murder:

	Bihari Convicts		Bengal Convicts	
Crimes	No	%	No	%
Burglary	4	3.8	26	2.8
Dacoity/gang robbery	47	45.2	295	31.8
Highway robbery	13	12.5	179	19.3
Murder	6	5.8	28	3
Robbery	20	19.2	154	16.6
" by open violence	13	12.5	179	19.3
Theft	0	0	29	3.1
Other	1	1	19	2
TOTALS	**104**	**100**	**928**	**100**

Source: India Office Library 'P' series convict indents

In addition, a number of the Bihari convicts had been involved in a violent insurrection at Alipur Jail in 1816, where convicts were sent to await their transportation. Several prisoners and guards were killed during this outbreak. Reflecting the serious nature of their offences, most of the Bihari convicts (78) were tattooed on the forehead with their names, crimes and dates of sentence, in the vernacular *Nagree* character. This process, known as *godna (godena)* was a measure designed to facilitate their recognition as convicts and to prevent their escape.

Bihari convicts in Mauritius

Sent out to work in small labouring parties all over the island, the Bihari convicts quickly became integrated into Mauritian social and economic life. The convicts were not segregated from the wider community and became involved in familial and religious affairs, as well as economic activity. There is no evidence that Bihari convicts maintained a separate identity from other convicts, social, religious, linguistic or otherwise. Like all convicts on the island, they quickly learned to speak the *lingua franca* of the island, Creole. They also married and had children, with slaves, creoles or other Indians. Convicts in general eventually disappeared, without trace, into the wider community.

By 1847, when the Colonial Office ordered an enquiry into the convicts in Mauritius, a number of Bihari convicts were still alive. Augund Korie was in good health. Aged about 25 when transported in 1815, he had become a skilled stonecutter and was employed as a Commander (a role similar to *sirdar*) in charge of convict working parties. Bodesing Gowallah was employed as a mason; Bhuttou Dosaud as a servant to the Surveyor General. Other Bihari convicts, including Ramah, were employed as Post Office Couriers, a common occupation for convicts at this time.

Other Bihari convicts did not fare so well. Fugurchund died of dysentery at the Camp de la Plaine des Roches, in 1838. Jhuree was sent to Diego Garcia in 1840, where all leprous slaves and convicts were banished at this time. Another Bihari named Bhuttou was run over by a cart in 1842 when working in Bain des Negresses. He had both legs amputated and was put to work as a basket maker. Tulluck Chund was murdered in 1837, having been robbed of the considerable amount of cash he had managed to accumulate during his time as a convict. The man tried for the crime (also a convict) was acquitted through lack of evidence.

कालापानी

बाँध ले गईले मोर प्यारे बलमा को जुलमी अंग्रेजवा
चिट्ठियाँ हम भेजत रहीं अंडमान कभी निकोवार के कैदवा
पर ना होवे मोर सजना अंडमान के द्वीपवा में हाय
और ना ही ऊ होवे निकोवार के जेलवा में भी हाय
भारत माता को मुक्ति दिलावे के ख्रातिर हे रामा
अंग्रेजन से बगावत कर जाने के ख्रातिर हे रामा
मोर बलमा को हाय हो गईल कालापानी का सजावा
मोर लोरवा ना सूखे अब ना करे जीने को मेरा मनवा
दिनवा लागे महीना जैसन लम्बा महीना लागे बरिसवा
बलमा के दुख दरदवा को सोच-सोच हमको न आवे नींदवा
जूलमवा से त भरल ही रहले बिदेसन के ई रजवा
अब काहे न कोई हमके भी पहुँचा दे मारीच के देसवा
मोर बलमा को हाय हो गईल कालापानी का सजवा
उधर काली पानी का सजवा इधर जिंदा मौत के दरदवा

The poem '**Kalapani**' by Abhimanyu Unnuth depicts the sorrow of a wife who has been separated from her husband. He has been sentenced to transportation as a convict - effectively a sentence of life imprisonment - for having rebelled against the British. Thinking that he is at the Andaman and Nicobar Islands where convicts were usually sent, she addresses letters to the authorities there asking for information about her husband. Receiving no answer, she decides to leave for Mauritius, crossing the 'black waters' or 'kalapani' herself, and joining her husband in the prison of exile.

The Bihari convicts were succeeded by a much greater immigration of indentured Indians brought to meet the island's increasing demand for labour in the developing plantation economy. Like the larger Bihari community which followed them to Mauritius, the fate of the convicts was mixed. A few prospered, while others fared less well. Most stayed on the island, integrating into the Creole and Indian populations and ultimately disappeared without trace.

Sources and Guide for Further Reading

The research for this article was carried out principally at the India Office Library and the Public Records Office, London and at the Mauritius Archives. For a more detailed account of the convict system in Mauritius see the author's *Convicts in the Indian Ocean: Transportation from South Asia to Mauritius, 1815-1853*, Macmillan, London, 2000. An article by the author on the tattooing of Indian convicts in Mauritius can be found in J. Kaplan (ed) *Written on the Body*, Reaktion, London, 2000.

A convict at work

I left life in the darkness of my garb, day I stab
And grab like all other prisoners. Janaab,
My black skin has robbed the sunlight again.
Their pain forces my forehead on their slabs.
They whip my shoulders, bruise my dreams in vain.
Gaya is my white beard, Dumka my whispers.
On every stone is engraved each of my tears!

Khal Torabully

The Characteristics of Bihari Recruits

Saloni Deerpalsingh

Much has been written on the historical literature of the indenture system and the different phases of Indian settlement but there exists a lacuna in the background information of the regional origins of the indentured recruits. This chapter emphasises the roots of those thousands of Biharis - men, women and children - whose circumstances compelled them to cross the *Kalapani* in quest of a better livelihood.

The beginnings of overseas migration from Bihar

When the British were looking for a labour force to replace slaves after the abolition of that trade in humans, Bihar proved to be a ready source for the supply of workers for the sugar colonies. Predominantly based on an agrarian economy, the populous state of Bihar was facing severe socio-economic problems by the mid 19th century. Internal British policies including the revenue and land settlements, the moneylenders' regulation Act, and changes to tenant rights in Bengal and Bihar which benefited dominant proprietary farmers, had serious social repercussions for the mass of the rural poor, leading to an increase in indebtedness and dependency. At the same time, British policies also acted to the detriment of local artisans and manufacturers, adding weavers and other craftsmen to the ranks of the unemployed and underemployed. To the usual migrant workers looking for seasonal work, were added the landless poor and the out-of-work artisans. The rise of export-oriented industries pushed many of these new migrants towards specific regions, such as Calcutta. According to Ranajit Das Gupta, the rapid expansion of the jute industry in Bengal drew an *"enormous flow of people from Bihar, Orissa and the united provinces to the metropolitan area"*. Large numbers of people from Bihar who came to Calcutta for permanent or temporary employment in mills and houses were lured by job opportunities *"ushered in by industrialisation"* and worked as *"coolies"*.

Natural calamities such as drought and harvest failures which brought famines in their wake, turned the steady stream of migrants into a flood. It was little wonder, then, that the colonial labour exporters should choose Calcutta to set up their agencies. The colonial depots which lined the River Hughli rapidly became a magnet for those who left behind starving and bereft villagers. Crossing the *"kalapani"* seemed, to these early migrants, the only solution.

The Biharis who embarked for Mauritius were initially from amongst those internal migrants who had come down to Bengal proper for various causes already enumerated. They were known as up-country migrants, a term still in use today. As the indenture system matured, many were recruited from their own districts in Bihar and taken to Calcutta accompanied by local recruiters known as *arkatis* and *duffadars* or by returnee migrants.

At the depot in Calcutta, and on arrival in Mauritius, the British assigned an immigration number to the recruit and recorded the place of origin, caste, age, next of kin and physical details of every individual in administrative registers. A duplicate of this information, together with details of employer were given to the immigrants in the form of a ticket. For as long as he or she was in the colony, this *"bond of identification"* was attached to the immigrant and had to be produced for all official purposes.

Migration Statistics

According to J. Geoghegan who conducted an enquiry into Indian migration in the 1870s: *"64% of the indentured labourers came mainly from North and of those who migrated from Calcutta from 1842 to 1870, the largest number came from Bihar ... about 40% of the total emigrants to Mauritius came from Bihar until 1890."* This clearly demonstrates the significance of the Biharis to the movement of indentured labour as a whole. This section evaluates the characteristics of the Bihari labourers introduced in the 19th Century through an analysis of statistical material.

Based on a sample of 2055 immigrants embarked between 1834 and 1843, three categories of Bihari immigrants were enumerated - Tribals, Muslims and Hindus. 106 of that total number, or 5%, were tribals, whilst 372 or 18%, were Muslim Biharis. Biharis of Hindu faith were the largest group, accounting for 948 or 46% of all indentured recruits during this period.

The Age of Bihari Migrants

Of 1423 Biharis who embarked at Calcutta before 1843, and whose age was enumerated, more than 50 % were aged between 21 and 30 years. The table below indicates the age range of Bihari immigrants introduced between 1834 and 1843.

Age groups of Biharis arriving in Mauritius between 1834 and 1843

Age	0-5	6-10	11-15	16-20	21-25	26-30	31-35	36-40	Above 40
No	3	7	19	199	316	473	265	90	51
%	0.2	0.5	1.3	14.0	22.2	33.2	18.6	6.3	3.6

Source: MGI, Indian Immigration Archive, PE 7

This preponderance of migrants aged between the late teens through to the early 30s, reflected the search for an able-bodied workforce by recruiters. This preference for young adults characterised the entire period of indentured recruitment, but as moves were made by the colonial state and by migrants themselves to introduce families, the age pyramids broadened. According to Marina Carter: *"the 21-25 age range was numerically the most significant between 1844 and 1857, although after that date a broader age distribution was noticeable with the rising numbers of families both nuclear and extended, immigrating".*

The Regional Origins of Bihari Migrants

Where do the Biharis settled in Mauritius come from? The migrants were from different strata of the rural population of the Bengal Presidency, which at that time included the provinces of Bihar and Uttar Pradesh. From the onset of indenture, the southern plains districts of Bihar, namely Arrah (Shahabad), Gaya (Sahebganj), Patna and the Chota Nagpur plateau (Hazaribagh), and Ranchi districts, provided the bulk of migrant labour to Mauritius. According to A. Sheel: *"In those parts of the districts of Shahabad and Gaya reliant on rainfall, agriculture was risky, and therefore it seems likely that until the early 70's, migration overseas was an attractive proposition for those displaced from their urban or industrial occupations or affected by vagaries of the seasons. Gaya and Shahabad suffered in the 1866 famine. Parts of Gaya were also affected by drought in 1869 ... people of these districts were living in difficult times in the period of colonial recruitment".*

The following divisions of the Bengal presidency, of which Bihar was a part in the 19th century sent the greatest number of migrants:

Bhagalpur Division	*Chota Nagpur Division*	*Patna Division*
Monghyr	Hazaribagh	Patna
Purnea	Ranchi	Gaya
Santal Parganas		Shahabad
		Saran
		Champaran
		Muzzafarpur
		Darbhanga

The migrants' region of origin was usually recorded in three separate columns which enumerated village, pergunnah and zillah. Most of the districts, places and villages ending in *"pur"*, *"pura"*, *"puri"*, *"nagar"*, *"gawa"*, *gawn"*, *"sahr"* mean town and village whereas names ending in *"garli"*, *"garhi"* means fort, and *"gang"* indicates a market. *"Sarai"* refers to an inn, *"putti"* a share of land, whilst those place-names ending with *"abad"* means inhabited or settled by.

The Ethnic Status of Bihari Migrants

(i) Tribals

The years 1843 and 1859 were the crucial years of labour importation. According to the Mauritius Almanach, these years witnessed the arrival of more than 17% of the labour force from India. Between 1843 and 1844, when tens of thousands of labourers embarked for Mauritius, many tribal migrants were among them, chiefly from Chota Nagpur division and the Santhal Pargana districts in South Bihar which have high concentrations of tribals. On the ship Northumberland which arrived in Mauritius on the 30th January 1843, out of a total of 231 immigrants embarked, 96 were tribals. The major tribal communities are commonly known as *"Santhal, Oraon, Munda, Ho"*. Some of the *"Oraons"* who are locally known as *"Dhangars"*, are located in West Champaran, and the Santhals in the districts of Purnea and Katihar.

Districts of Origin of Tribals

Palamu	North Chota Nagpur	Santhal Parganah	Other Divisions
Ranchi	Hazaribagh	Dumka	Rohtas
Gumla	Girindi	Godda	West Champaran
Lohardaga	Dhanbad	Deoghar	Purnea
East Singhbhum		Sahebganj	Katihar
West Singhbhum			Bhagalpur
			Manger

According to a British Indian official, at this time one third of the Indians going to Mauritius were *"Tribals"*. In the first decade of indenture, tribals were found on every ship leaving Calcutta. Other tribal groups arriving included Mundas and Gonds or Khonds. Further designations for tribals included Kharia, Bhumij, Banjara and Baiga. The regions of Nagpore, Ramghur and Hazareebaug predominated amongst a group of tribals who arrived in 1843 on the Northumberland. All recensed as Dangars, many of their names ended with the suffixes 'ram' or 'oo'; thus 'Ragoo', 'Bundhoo', 'Batchoo Ram', 'Rajah Ram' and 'Moteeram'. A small number of female tribals travelled with the group along with three children aged between 6 and 11.

After 1844, there were fewer immigrants from the Tribal group. Their heavy mortality in the unfamiliar epidemological environment of Calcutta and on board the ships which took them to Mauritius, discouraged the colonial authorities from actively recruiting them. However, some tribals continued to arrive on the island, throughout the period of indenture.

(ii) Muslims from Bihar

According to the Imperial Gazetteer, the 'Musalmans' of Bihar *"may be divided into three classes: Foreign tribes, Saiyid and descended from*

Radhaye, pictured here, was a tribal immigrant who migrated from Bihar in 1844 aboard the Appolline.

converted Hindus [some] retaining Hindu caste names. Julahas and Fakir are also chiefly of Hindu origin."

A large group of Muslim Biharis who embarked on the *Shah Allum* in February 1843 came from Chapra, Patna, Gya and Purneeah. Mmost had identifiably Muslim names: Hosseinbuks, Peerbux, Lalmohamed, Nazeer, Hakim Khan, Sheik Rumally and Sheik Golaup. A few bore traces of a Hindu origin: for example, Kumloo's father was named 'Ramjan' and another immigrant was named Jhubboo.

In fact, many Muslims bore traditional Bihari names ending in *"eea"*, *"oo"*, *"run"*, *"won"*, *"uth"*, *"ry"*, *"auth"*. This can be seen more clearly from the following extract of the register of arrival of the ship *Futtay Salem* in 1858 detailing a group of Muslim women from the regions of Arrah and Gaya:

Name of immigrant	Father's/Mother's name	Age	Region of origin
Jensee	Mutty	36	Arrah
Ustoornee	Subratty	46	Arrah
Aumearun	Seetakhan	40	Guya

Source: *Indian Immigration Archives, MGI*

Cheeneebacus, pictured here, was a Muslim from Bihar who migrated to Mauritius aboard the Charlotte in 1852.

(iii) The Bihari Hindus: Caste Data

Caste was once a signifier of a traditional occupation – it denoted less a community than a social stratum defined according to employment. J.C. Nesfield has written, "*The bond of sympathy or interest which first drew together the families or tribal fragments, of which caste is composed, was not, as some writers have alleged, community of creed or community of kinship, but community of function. Function ... was the foundation upon which the whole caste system of India was built up".*

The immigrants who settled in Mauritius were accurately recensed in caste terms and according to Marina Carter *"the principal caste groups migrating through Calcutta can be identified as Chamars, Kurmis, Gowalas, Dosads, and Koeris".*

This Hindu Bihari came to Maurititius in 1862.

Because of their preponderance, many members of the larger caste groupings were able to practice endogamous marriages so that these castes remain common today in Mauritius. Smaller numbers of high caste Brahmins and Rajputs (or Kshattry/Chattriya) also migrated. It is not always possible to distinguish caste from the name but some Rajputs can be identified by the 'Singh' suffix. Thus Sohunbersing, who arrived on the Shah Allum on 14 Feb 1843 listed his father's name as Seebasingh, and was a 36 year old 'Kshattry' from Arrah.

Classification of castes by traditional occupation

Caste	Occupation
Ahir	Herdsman and milkman
Bania	Merchant and moneylender
Bedar	Soldier and public service
Beldar	Digger
Bhoyar	Cultivator
Bhuinhar	Land owner
Brahmin	Priest
Cahar	Carrier
Chamar	Leather workers
Dangri	Vegetable-grower
Darzi	Tailor
Dhobi	Washerman
Dosaud	Village watchman
Dom	Supply fire for cremation
Gosain	Religious mendicant
Gowalla	Milkman and cattle breeders
Hajjam	Barber
Halwai	Confectioner / Grain parchers
Jat	Land owner and cultivator
Julaha	Weaver
Kahar	Palanquin bearer /Household servant
Kasai	Butcher
Kayasth	Village accountant, writer and clerk
Kewat	Boatman and fisherman
Koiry	Cultivator
Kshatriya	Warrior and land-owner
Kumhar	Potters
Kurmi	Cultivator
Lohar	Blacksmith
Mali	Gardener and vegetable grower
Mallah	Boatman and fisherman
Nai	Barber
Nunia	Salt-Refiner and digger
Ojha	Augur and Medium
Pasi	Toddy-drawer and labourer
Rajput	Soldier and land owner
Rangrez	Dyer
Sudh	Cultivator
Sunar	Goldsmith and silversmith
Teli	Oilman

The table opposite provides a list of some of the main North Indian castes and the traditional occupations ascribed to individuals belonging to that group.

The spoken dialect of Bihari Immigrants

The majority of Bihari migrants spoke Bhojpuri and Hindustani (the British term encompassing both Hindi and Urdu). Other vernaculars spoken by 19th century Biharis from specific regions are as follows:

Patna	*Chota Nagpur*	*Bhagalpur*
Maithili	Magahi	Bengali
Jolahaboli	Santali	Rarhiboli
Bhojpuri	Rarhiboli	Bihari
Awadhi	Ho, Bengali, Oriya,	Maithili
Madesi	Santali and Mudari	Chhika chikhi boli
Shekoi		Santali
Musalmani		Maghdhi
Magahi		Hindi

According to Ramyead, *"the language of the great majority of Indian immigrants arriving since 1834 was Bhojpuri. There must have been small dialectal differences in the Bhojpuri spoken by Biharis hailing from different parts of the vast province of Bihar, and somewhat wider differences in the Bhojpuri of the Biharis and that of the immigrants originating from the North Western provinces"*.

Ramyead also offers an interpretation of the evolution of language use amongst Bihari immigrants as they established themselves on Mauritius: *"The arbitrary settlement of immigrants on estate camps, with mobility confined to limited areas, led, it must be conjectured, to a homogenisation of the Indian community, and parallel with this movement, their dialect differences too, must have undergone a process of homogenisation. The consequence was the evolution of a more or less standardised and mutually intelligible language, a unified Bhojpuri, spoken by a people who had grown socially and culturally very much analogous. It was the beginning of the formation of the Mauritian Bhojpuri of today, not identical to any one single Bhojpuri dialect in India. By 1900, the general pattern of Mauritian Bhojpuri spoken all over the island was already firmly set."*

Sources and Guide for Further Reading

The statistical data used for the preparation of this article derive primarily from the Indian Immigration Registers held at the Mahatma Gandhi Institute, Mauritius. These records are a unique frame of reference for the researcher and a useful genealogical tool for Biharis and others wishing to trace their ancestors in Mauritius. *The Imperial Gazetteers*, Government of India, Vols. II, III, IV, XXIV provide helpful background material about socio-economic conditions in the different regions of 19th century Bihar. The principal secondary sources used for further background information on Bihar include Sharma A. N. 'Nature and extent of migration in Bihar', 1994, Das Gupta R. *Factory labour in Eastern India*, and Sheel A. 'Long term demographic trends in South Bihar: Gaya and Sahabad districts' in *The Indian Economic and Social History Review*, 29, 1992. For material on Bihari immigrants in Mauritius, Carter M., *Servants, Settlers and Sirdars, 1995* and Deerpalsingh S. & Carter M., *Select Documents on Indian Immigration* were consulted. Ramyead L. P. *The establishment and cultivation of modern standard hindi in Mauritius*, 1985, is indispensable as a guide to the languages spoken by Bihari migrants.

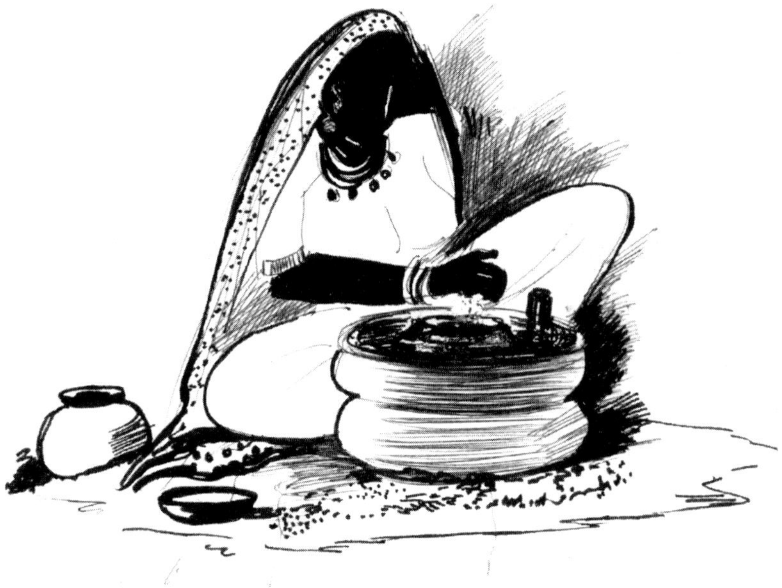

Weaving Destiny

Au ghat, la patience repoussera l'exil
Très loin, car nos mains tissent déjà nos destinées.

Khal Torabully

The Journey of Bihari Indentured Labourers

V. Govinden

The long journey of indentured labour began with the freeing of slaves. The servile labourers of Mauritius became apprentices on 1st February 1835. Apprenticeship was a half-way house between slave and wage labour, designed to ease the path to full abolition, and required slaves to work for a further few years with their owners. In the immediate aftermath of slavery, the British government was determined to prevent its perpetuation in new forms. By an Order in Council of 7th September 1838 the former slave colonies were required to appoint Stipendiary Magistrates to administer justice impartially to the employers and their labourers. A series of other reforms did nothing, however, to convince the apprentices to remain in field labour as free men and women, whilst they increased the apprehensions of their employers. As the days of apprenticeship ran out many former slaves downed tools and prepared to leave the plantations. Most planters were not willing to bargain with those who remained, or to entice back those who had departed.

The planters were already turning to the millions of India who they believed could be induced to labour in the canefields at a cost no greater than that expended on the slaves. Agents in Calcutta offered the prospect of 'hill coolies', men attracted to the port with its opportunities for seasonal employment, and soon to the be lured onto the ships bound for Mauritius and other British colonies. During the 1840s and 1850s these tribals, also known as 'dangars', formed a sizeable proportion of those taken overseas under indenture. The thousands who shouldered their little bundles and marched away found the strength to sever the ties with home only because they believed that they would, quite soon, be back again.

The Recruitment of Bihari Labourers

One of the first recorded contracts made for Bihari tribals going to Mauritius was that entered into by 151 coolies of Dhangur caste, with Messrs Lyall Matheson & Co., agents of Mr John Shaw Sampson, in 1831. The agreement stated that the labourers would,

> *for and during the term of 5 years commencing from the day of the date of their departure from Calcutta for the island of Mauritius, to be accounted and fully to be complete, to faithfully truly and diligently serve the said John Shaw Sampson or such other person or persons to whom their services may by the said John Shaw Sampson by transferred, as labourers for the purpose of cultivating sugar, tending cattle, repairing roads and doing and performing all such usual and customary work as the custom and practice of labourers of the island of Mauritius warrants or prescribes and the said parties hereto of the second part do further undertake covenant ... to perform and execute such services aforesaid and not be absent therefrom except on good and sufficient cause from daylight to the evening of each and every day during the said term reserving such reasonable time for rest and food during the interim of work ... provided that such period shall not be less than two hours of each and every day ...*

The labourers were to be given daily as food "14 chitttacks of rice, 2 of dahl, one half of ghee and 2 of fish together with such other necessary food as is customary for natives of the same caste and religion as the said parties" and were also to be provided with 1 blanket, 2 dhoties, 1 chintz jacket, 1 lascar cap, 1 wooden bowl and 1 brass lota. The employer was also expected to provide medicine and medical attendance, and a free return passage. The pay was to be 5 rupees monthly. With some modifications, these terms were to form the basis for thousands of indenture contracts over the century.

The tribals were found to be good workers in Mauritius, and as more labourers were required, the recruiters' catchment area widened. By the mid 19th century the suitability of Biharis for estate labour was widely recognised. The Protector of Immigrants in Mauritius preferred Bihari to Bengali migrants, stating that emigrants from Jessor, Kishnagor and districts in the immediate vicinity of Calcutta were "inferior in physical strength and in agricultural knowledge, to those who come from Gya, Patna, Arrah, Gazeepore and Benares. Those who proceed from Bancoorah, Hazareebagh and the hilly districts become the steadiest and best labourers".

By 1861 when the Protector of Immigrants made that report, migration to Mauritius had become common in Bihar. Many villagers had frends or relations on the island. But in the 1830s, the first recruits had little idea of where they were being sent. This was confirmed by a Bihari, Ramdeen, who was interviewed at Calcutta Town Hall on 10 December 1840, shortly after completing an indenture contract. He described a voyage made to Mauritius five years previously, with a group of 250 *coolies*, 50 of whom were 'dangahs', and who had been told that they were 'engaged to do the Company's work', considering this to mean work for the Indian government.

Some Bihari recruits were literally kidnapped and confined at recruiters' houses until embarkation. At the house of Srikissen *babu*, in late 1830's Calcutta, Sergeant Floyd discovered several *godowns* containing up-country *coolies* who informed him that they had been kept in a state of close captivity: "they satisfied the calls of nature attended by a couple of burkendauzes ... some of the men were chastised almost daily with strokes from shoes".

Even those Biharis who wanted to join family and friends who had already migrated to Mauritius, might find themselves duped and disappointed. Another return migrant, Jhurry, told the Mauritian Protector of Immigrants in 1861: "My brother left Arrah to come and join me. He was enticed away by an Arkotty who took him to the Trinidad Depot. I endeavoured to communicate with my brother, but was prevented by the Arkotty who had charge of him. I have heard that my brother has been sent away to Trinidad".

Kalash

An earthen vessel which represents the embodiment of the whole universe.

The Kalash is usually associated with ritual transitions

Embarkation Procedures at the Emigration Depot in Calcutta

On arrival at the Mauritius Emigration Depot located at Bhawanipur in Calcutta, new emigrants were required to bathe and received an issue of clothing, their old ones being washed and returned. The medical inspection by the Indian doctor in the case of the men and by 2 nurses for the women followed. Women were not subjected to a searching physical examination lest this would scare away potential female recruits. In the 1870's, the nurse's examination was still superficial but by the end of the nineteenth century a more rigorous procedure had been adopted. After the men were passed by the Indian doctor, they had to appear before a European depot surgeon and also before a government doctor nominated by the Protector of Emigrants.

Any coolie who was not suffering from an obvious malformation or displaying evidence of disease would pass the doctor. The Emigration Agent had paid out a full commission to the recruiter, and was under pressure to fill a ship and despatch the emigrants as speedily as possible. The only person concerned who had a motive to scrutinize the recruits rigorously was the surgeon superintendent who was responsible for delivering them alive, and if possible well, at the end of the voyage. The surgeon superintendent was required to sign a certificate that the coolie was in good health when coming on board; it was therefore in his interest to verify conditions properly. However, unless he was a senior man, and exceptionally firm in asserting himself, he was likely to be pressed to pass many for embarkation who were not fit to go.

The Protector of Immigrants at Mauritius who inspected arriving recruits decried the poor health of many who entered his depot. His comments on those disembarked from the Winifred in 1845 are revealing: "from the squalid and attenuated appearance of some of those who reached their destination here, I am led to imagine that aged and debilitated persons of both sexes, unfit for any useful purpose in the colony, may have been permitted to embark on this occasion.... Every expense incurred for the introduction of several males and females by the 'Winifred' is an utter loss to the colony. In a report to the Governor the Protector drew attention to the fact that some of those on board had had to be sent to the hospital immediately, while 7 men, 3 women and a boy had died on the passage itself. One of the men sent to the hospital as extremely sick was only 22 years old - and was a Bramin from Bhagalpur in Bihar. Other Biharis arriving on the ship included a 40 year old Kahar woman, 2 'Moondas' or tribals, and a young Koiry male.

When the day came for the emigrants to leave the depot and embark on the ship, the Protector of Emigrants was present to see them aboard. Each emigrant was issued with a pass and a "tin ticket" which was tied around the neck or strapped to the arm.

The Sea Voyage to Mauritius

The real trial of the emigrants began on the voyage. On the high seas for at least 30-35 days, their patience and stamina were put to a severe test. Many could not overcome homesickness and others could not bear the strain of a long sea journey, which they had not experienced before. Because the great majority of emigrants were country folk, leaving their villages often for the first time, the passage presented many problems for them, in regard to food, water, living space, medical care and the officer's treatment towards them.

The unfamiliarity of sea life and ship's diet was described by a British official in 1845:

> *On first quitting India the natives are utterly unacquainted with the nature of a sea voyage, and quite incapable in every way of providing for its wants. The natural solicitude of the Supreme Government of India to protect their subjects has established regulations which require the ships to supply provisions of such varied description as natives of the "immigrant class" have been but little accustomed to.*

Arrival of a 'Coolie Ship' at Aapravasi Ghat

Ravis d'avoir traversé l'eau noire, ils bénirent l'eau
Au bout du voyage. La mer est repos et péril!
Vivre enfin ici, au pays à cultiver ...
Avant de creuser son ventre de terre fertile
Silence et attente seront nos proches assemblées:
Il nous faut espérer entre les murs du dépôt!

Khal Torabully

In these early years of indenture, many irregularities were discovered in the records of ships' captains. Age and caste of emigrants were not properly entered, the emigrants that died during the period of embarkation were replaced by others, and the formalities of embarkation were frequently neglected - coolies were shipped at the same time, and in different vessels, as procured from crimps and the list was closed on the last day only. Bheck Roy, a male Dangur who arrived in Mauritius in July 1845, was remarked on by the Protector, who wrote: *"The age of "Bheck Roy" appears to me to be about 65 years, although he is described in his certificate as 41, and he certainly is unfit for field labour in this colony."* It may be concluded that many of the Biharis sent to Mauritius in the first decade of indentured migration were both unwilling and unfit for plantation work.

On board the ship, emigrants were allocated a specific living space. Act XIII of 1864 expressly provided that women and children were to occupy a compartment separate from that of single men. The single women were berthed aft, in the rear section of the ship, the married couples and children were accommodated between them and the single men, the largest group, were put in the forward part of the ship. All were required in moderate weather to come on the upper deck daily and to remain on deck at least one hour. The dispensary was placed on the top deck, and a hospital and cook-house were also set up on board. This was the world of the emigrants for many weeks and months.

From 1861 Medical Officers in charge of emigrant ships were required to maintain a diary of the medical history of the voyage, and the proportion of women to men was regulated. Passage conditions improved to some extent in the 1880s and efforts to introduce steamers cut down the length of the voyage by the 1890s.

This did not prevent trouble from breaking out periodically on 'coolie ships'. Migrants rebelled when their womenfolk were ill-treated, when living conditions were poor and when the regimentation of shipboard life became unbearable. On 18 April 1874, some coolies aboard the

Allum Ghir, led by one Balgobin, refused to go up on deck to eat their food and called upon their shipmates to return below decks. The Master ordered his crew to remove the ladders to prevent the coolies going down, only to see them mobbed. When order was eventually restored, the ringleaders, adjudged to be Bengalia and Gya, were handcuffed. Those who refused to accept deprivation and ill-treatment on the voyage made their voices heard in such ways throughout the period of indentured migration.

Mortality at sea was another serious problem for ships' captains and crews. The outbreak of epidemic diseases such as cholera or smallpox could decimate the passengers in the confined space of the ship. Cases of serious disease on board could also mean that a ship might be forced into quarantine, entailing weeks and months in makeshift accommodation at quarantine stations. Some deaths on the voyage were self-inflicted: attempts at suicide by jumping overboard were relatively common.

Those first Bihari migrants who survived the arduous sea passage to tell their story revealed that they had been incited and encouraged to emigrate by recruiters who informed them that the colony of Mauritius, which was known in North India as "Mirich Desh", was close to the mainland. It was only when the ship had sailed off that they were told of its real distance and the length of the voyage, and that they would not be able return home until after five years of service. In later years when the migrants had more understanding of the terms and conditions of servitude, death still stalked the ships and sea sickness brought down the morale of the most hardy. The coolies, like the slaves before them, nevertheless gained something positive from their voyage – fortitude, and a sense of comradeship and brotherhood for those, known as *jehaji-bhai*, who had shared the passage with them.

Sources and Guide for Further Reading

The RA series of the Mauritius Archives and the various Indian immigration registers held at the Mahatma Gandhi Institute have been used for the preparation of this article. H. Tinker's *A New System of Slavery*, Oxford, 1974, remains an absorbing read for students of the indenture system generally. M. Carter's *Servants, Sirdars and Settlers*, OUP, 1995, covers the sea voyage to Mauritius specifically.

Life under Indenture: Bihari Migrants' Stories

Marina Carter

Despite the deceptions and disappointments which often accompanied the journey into the unknown and resulted from the low status of the 'coolie', the indentured labourers who arrived from Bihar cannot simply be seen as the unhappy victims of an unfair and brutalising system. Most of the men and women who formed the nucleus of the 19th century sugar estate camps worked hard to overcome the difficulties of their exile and to improve their lot in life. This is the story of their struggle, and who better to tell this story than the indentured Biharis themselves?

Itinerant Labourers and the Money Motive

Most of the Biharis who came to Mauritius did so because they were tempted by offers of high wages. Many were already away from home looking for work when they were recruited. For some, the money wage was dangled, but the whereabouts of the job was kept secret.

Karoo of Khurkotta in the district of Monger, vividly recalled the words of the recruiter who came into his neighbourhood:

He asked us: 'What are you doing in the jungle? Come to Calcutta, and you will get employment for repairing roads, for which you will receive pay at the rate of four rupees per month, besides diet'. We came; he paid all our expenses on the road. When we arrived here, he told us that no employment on the roads could be got: 'You had better go forward and you will find plenty of employment'. He mentioned that we should go to the Mauritius, and said it was a good country, and that we should get good food and good clothes there. ... I got two months' pay

> *at Mauritius, eight rupees; after which I became ill .... When I was cured I was sent to the police, and the magistrate asked me if I wished to return home; I told him I wished to return to Calcutta; he said 'Very well; go'.*

Karoo's experience in Mauritius had been brief and disease-ridden. Some did not even get that far. Gholam Ally of Chapra was looking for his brother in Calcutta when he was recruited in 1838. The recruiter's godown was raided, and Ally decided to leave before he was embarked for Mauritius. He gave this statement to the Calcutta Magistrate before returning home:

> *I am a resident of Dowlutgunge, in Chupprah, and am a cultivator; I have a father and brothers at home; I have a brother here who is a syce in some service; I could not find him, but fell in with Bhowant Singh, who asked me whether I would go to the Mauritius; I said I would; that was seven days ago; I lived in a place near Brijitalao provided by Bhowanny; he gave us food; five days ago a number of people, two gentlemen and a great multitude of people surrounded me, and inquired who had brought us and asked for the name of the duffadar; ... I was let go; they said they would give me 10 rupees to send me home.*

The desire to better their lot and to earn a decent wage was the most important factor in determining migrants' decisions to come to Mauritius. Many Biharis went in groups and the degree of organisation was prodigious. The account of Raghoonath, a Dhangur from Bihar, of how he recruited a group of men and took them overseas demonstrates the degree to which even the supposedly simple 'hill coolies' could take charge of the transportation of labourers. Some of those in his band were recruited at Chota Nagpore, others at Bancoorah, still more in Calcutta itself. Men like Raghoonath were not victims - they were opportunists. He told his story as follows:

> *I am of the Dhangur caste; I went five years ago in charge of 50 of my countrymen to the Mauritius through the house of Gillanders & Co; our names were registered at the Calcutta police; Ramanauth, sirdar, of my caste, wrote to me telling me the terms of service at the Mauritius; I brought away the 50 men; I have brought 300 rupees with me ... I have money enough for my son; I left behind me a wife and two sons; one of 13 years and one of 8 years of age at that time; there was no danger of their being starved – I sent my advance of 36 rupees to them.... Our men of course will pay what their relations have expended on their families; Muhajuns would advance on that account to the relations.*

Raghoonath's account reveals the means by which single male migrants would support their families while away, or refund the moneylenders on their return. Juggurnath, one of the men who went to Mauritius with Raghoonath, also a Dhangur, explained why he emigrated: "I used to cultivate land in Chota Nagpore. I have brought back 294 rupees - I could never save any money from my old trade as cultivator. I took my wife and four children with me, and they are all returned, and two more are born who have come with me also - their passage was paid by Monsieur Rudelle, my master - I paid for their food."

Raghoonath's band were from diverse backgrounds - Girdharee stated "I come from Patna and was a shopkeeper there, I could not get employment and so went to Mauritius". High caste Biharis were amongst the band. Evidently, the need to earn a living was more significant than differences in status. Shewchurn described himself and his experience of migration in these terms:

> *I am a Patna Elwar Bramin. I used to cultivate the soil at Phoolwaree; I came down for employment as a durwan. I met Raghoonath and engaged with him for Mauritius. I was injured there and unable to work for three years; in the last two years I have earned and brought away 40 rupees ... if I was slow at work I used to get a slap on my posterior with a cane.*

A Life of Toil

History turning a blind eye bore him not witness
History standing mute told not his full story
He who first had watered this land with his sweat
And turned stone into green fields of gold
The first immigrant He, son of this land
He was mine, he was yours, he was our very own

Abhimanyu Unnuth

Evidently Shewchurn had not had a very fruitful stay in Mauritius. His statement reveals that even those at the top of the caste system were not necessarily averse to crossing the *kalapani* to earn a living. Rade Sing, of Chupra, was a Rajput by caste, and returned from Mauritius at the age of 30 after serving out his contract there. He had left home as a ten year old boy, and had lived a wandering life since then, even working as a *lathial*, or bodyguard.

The lives of Biharis such as the 50 men who were recruited by and accompanied Raghoonath to Mauritius were inevitably transformed by their migration. Burgee, a Dhangar of Chota Nagpore, brought more than money home from Mauritius. He reported: "I fell in with Raghoonath in Calcutta; I married my wife at the Mauritius – she has returned – she is the daughter of one of the Coolies ... I have only 80 rupees, I have been 10 months married – it cost me 20 rupees".

The Hard Graft of Plantation Labour

One of the most frequent comments of new Bihari recruits, as with other Indian immigrants, was that the work expected by the Mauritian employers was harder than the labour customarily required at home. The routine and discipline of the sugar estate, and the sheer graft expected of a cane cutter came as a shock to many. Some were simply not fit enough to be able to bear the brunt of the daily slog. The result could be a vicious cycle of absenteeism and punishment. Rughoo, a Bramin from Arrah, found himself out of favour with his employer because of absenteeism, and then in difficulties with buying himself free from the indenture contract:

> *I went to the roll call at 4.30 on Saturday before last and my master Mr Rondeau was angry with me because I had been absent from work for 4 days. He struck me with his umbrella on the chest. ... He then told me that I was not fit for the work on the estate and that I had better refund to him the money I had cost the estate and*

he would have my engagement cancelled. I asked permission on Sunday to be allowed to go for the money to redeem my industrial residence. Leave was refused me and I therefore left the estate without leave and stayed away on Sunday and Monday. At the roll call on Tuesday I offered Rs 160, which I had been able to borrow, to Mr Rondeau. He refused to accept the money and sent me to my work, taking me by the nape of the neck and pushing me to the place where I was to work. I worked for a little while and then absented myself. I went to the head office in town to report my request for the cancelling of my contract. I was given a letter for Mr Rondeau. On reading the letter Mr Rondeau told me to bring Rs 200 and he would cancel my contract. I have had much difficulty in collecting the Rs 160 above mentioned and am unable to get more. I ask the Protector to intervene on my behalf.

The Protector did intervene in favour of Rughoo. Finding that the Bihari's cost of introduction amounted to Rs 155.50 with rations, that official calculated he had cost the estate only Rs 158.25. Rondeau was asked to accept this amount and Rughoo was released from the obligation to fulfil an 'industrial residence' on 14 November 1883. He remained in the colony for a further ten years, before returning to India in September 1893.

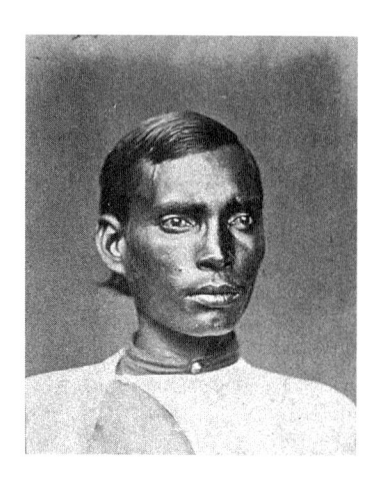

Rughoo arrived on the Merchantman in 1893, but this was not his first visit to Mauritius. He was a returnee – this Bramin from Arrah had adopted the guise of a new immigrant which helps to explain how he was able to buy himself out of his indenture so quickly.

If those Biharis who found plantation labour too arduous often had difficulty in cancelling their indentures, immigrants who were owed wages were equally disadvantaged. The courts were notoriously biased in favour of employers, but persistent litigants could receive judgments in their favour. On the 3rd November 1898, Hossenbuccus no 336,140, a watchman, sued his employer for one year's arrears of wages - amounting to Rs 156 - and judgment was given in his favour for the amount claimed. However, his debtor was in prison and had no goods which could be sold to pay his creditors. Hossenbuccus accordingly sought the assistance of an agent, Mr G Faduilhe, of Quatre Bornes. Faduilhe arranged for the sale of property owned by the debtor, Mamode Syed Ally, in Rose Hill. This sale fetched Rs 1250 in 1898. By February 1900, Hossenbucus, now living at Ebene, Stanley, where he was under written engagement to the estate as a cane cutter, had still not been paid, having only received the sum of fifteen rupees from Faduilhe. The young Bihari Muslim from Patna who had come to Mauritius in 1868 as a 20 year old, was still working on the estates more than 30 years later. His life of unremitting labour ended at Ebene in 1926.

Hossenbuccus

The Rights of Old Immigrants

The famous petition of old immigrants, drawn up in 1871 at the behest of a sympathetic planter, Adolphe de Plevitz, drew attention to the plight of those Indians who, having successfully completed their indenture contracts and, settling on the island as small planters or traders in their own right, were subjected to continual harrassment by the police. Hundreds of old immigrants had rallied at collection points around the island to affix their signatures to the document written on their behalf. The grievances of sixteen individuals were highlighted in the petition eventually submitted to the Governor. Several of these were Biharis. Two of their stories, as they appeared in the petition, are detailed below.

Budha, Old Immigrant No.180,788, who resided on the estate of M. Tessier in Nouvelle Decouverte, recounted how he had been forced out of his home one night by police engaged in a 'vagrant hunt'. Budha was from the district of Ranchi in Bihar and had arrived in Mauritius as a 28 year old in 1857. He was a Muslim.

About a year ago, during the night, hearing a noise of voices in my yard, and going out to see what was the matter, I found my house, as well as those of my neighbours, surrounded by constables; they entered into our houses, and compelled us to come out of them. They then asked us for our tickets and police passes. We were 32 in number, and had our photograph tickets, the leases for the ground we occupied, and our police passes for the district of Pamplemousses, in which district, as our leases showed, we resided; notwithstanding which we were forcibly tied two by two and marched from our homes and our hard-earned property, some of us leaving our wives and children weeping with grief; others, who had but little furniture, gardener's tools, and some fowls, and no one to take care of them during their absence, were obliged to leave them at the mercy of any evilly-disposed persons. This occurred on a Saturday. We were taken to Moka, locked up there from that day *until Monday at 10 am, when we were taken before the Magistrate ... Having no idea what the law was or might be, we clubbed together to procure legal advice, at the rate of $1 per man ... our case was remitted four days three times consecutively; after which we were released. We had thus travelled backwards and forwards about 200 miles, having to suffer expenses, and some of us the total loss of our property.*

The presentation of the petition to the Governor was attended with widespread publicity on the island and contributed to the decision to send a Royal Commission to investigate the conditions of Indian labourers in Mauritius. Heavy criticism of police tactics by the petitioners led to the setting up of an internal enquiry into the conduct of the police. The results of this were published in 1872. The police commented on each of the 16 cases highlighted in the petition. On the grievance of Budha, the report admitted that he "was a victim to the overzeal of the police, as with all his papers in regular order, he was captured, or rather taken a prisoner (in a vagrant hunt) while in his own domicile, and forcibly taken to the police station". Mr Tessier, the lawyer who had defended the men, and also the proprietor of their land, did not support Budha's statement that any property of the victims had been lost as a result. He did, however, report that Budha and his neighbours "suffered great inconvenience from a practice of the police, to come at night to their premises" and stated his belief that "unless the police were in possession of warrants to do so, they had no right to enter the huts of honest and industrious men, or to search their premises". Perhaps Budha was the victim of further harrassment as a result of the publicity his case generated, or perhaps he simply tired of his life in Mauritius, for he returned to India a few years later, in November 1875.

Madhoo, No 46,079 of Long Mountain, was a Santhal tribal who had been an early immigrant to Mauritius, arriving in 1844 at the age of 30. His grievance related to his arrest whilst attempting to visit a sick friend.

Evening at the Estate Camp

On or about the 20th of April, 1871, I was informed that my friend Mungor, residing at Vacoas, was very ill. Accordingly I started on the following Friday to visit him, and arrived by train at the Beau Bassin Station, where I was arrested by a constable and locked up ... once before the Magistrate I explained what had happened to me, and the reasons thereof. I was not condemned, but was locked up until the following Monday, when being again taken before him I was liberated the same day at 4 pm. I am 57 years of age and have resided in the colony for about 35 years. I have always served my employers faithfully, and never been condemned for absence from my duties.

When the Police Inquiry Commission attempted to investigate Madhoo's grievance - they could not trace his whereabouts. Perhaps Madhoo had realised that his best course of action was to 'disappear' and shake off the notoriety of being one of the most talked-about subjects of the infamous 'Petition'. Other Biharis simply tried to circumvent the harsh laws through fair means or foul. Puteeram, a Bihari of Sonar caste from Arrah, who arrived in Mauritius in 1865 as a 15 year old, passed himself off as an old immigrant by 'borrowing' the ticket of another man. This was a common ruse to escape detection if a labourer had deserted from an estate, or simply wished to move elsewhere. Puteeram, however, was detected and prosecuted in 1882 for "using a ticket which did not rightfully apply to him".

Old Immigrant's Ticket.

DUPLICATE

Name of Immigrant .... Teeluck
Number 237529
Name of Father............... Bheenick
Name of Mother............... Jacoty
Age (in letters) .... Forty
Stature (in feet and inches)... 5 Feet
Caste .... Dosad
Marks.........................
Native Country .... Arrah
Number of Vessel by which introduced 876

This Immigrant is free to engage himself.

Delivered this 22d April 186 7.

In absence of the Protector of Immigrants.

Chief Clerk.

Migrants who had completed their indenture contracts had to carry their tickets at all times, to avoid harrassment from the police. This is the ticket of Teeluck, a Dosaud from Arrah in Bihar.

The Return Home

Immigrants who were found guilty of offences against the labour laws such as that committed by Puteeram would be given a short prison sentence and returned to the estate. Serial offenders, however would be sent back to India. The colony had no use for persistent runaways who were labelled 'incorrigible vagabonds' and put on a ship home. The most determined rebels even used this as an avenue of escape. Rampoorsad, from Saran in Bihar, arrived in 1889, and requested a free passage home in 1895. He was found to be wanted at Flacq on a charge of larceny and was sentenced to 12 months imprisonment. On 24 July 1896, however, Rampoorsad was given his wish. He was registered for a free passage to Calcutta and the Protector ordered that he be fed in the depot and that a *cumlie* and a tin plate be given to him. A letter was sent to the Calcutta Agent and a photograph of Rampoorsad was pasted in the register. He had been labelled a vagrant, and the colony had no wish to see him return to the island.

Immigrants who knew their way around the system would assist their fellow Indians to obtain free passages home – at a price. Bethul, a Bihari of the Kahar caste from Gya, was one such man. He had come to Mauritius as a 30 year old in 1864 and in 1896 he inveigled Chummun, who had come to the depot at Port Louis to enquire about a return passage, out of Rs 38.50. Chummun later complained that he had come to the Immigration Office to pay for his passage to India, bringing with him 82 rupees. Bethul, who was standing outside the Protector's office, told Chummun to hand over to him the amount and to swear before the Protector that he was unable to pay for his passage. Chummun did so, and obtained a free passage. However, when Chummun asked Bethul to give him back his money; Bethul returned only Rs 43.50 and walked away with the difference - Rs 38.50.

Other Biharis were sent home because they were unable to work and were considered to be a drain on the colony's resources. Subboo of Hazareebagh was sent away after working on a sugar estate for one year because he had been injured: "I was told that as I was disabled by the fall of a tree on my wrist, I had better return to my own country, and I was put on board ship".

Most migrants, however, returned to India because they had saved enough money and wished to see their families. Heengen, who worked as a domestic servant for a number of Mauritian families, decided to make the journey to India after learning that his father had died. His story, told on his return to Calcutta in 1841, is as follows:

> *I am a native of Behar, and have been to Mauritius for three years. I was a Khidmudgar before I went, and I was one at Mauritius ... I left my first master Mr Blondeau, because my master's relatives insisted upon my cleaning the floor of the house, which was of wood. ... I then went to Mr Missel Belownee; he is a writer in the government office; I stayed one year with him in great comfort, and got leave from him for six months; I will go back to him. I came here on account of my father's death; I have about 200 rupees with me. The passage down was very pleasant, only I was beat on the day I went on board about a girl, an ayah.*

Evidently, his years of working in Mauritian households had given Heengen a taste for lady's maids!

After the five years required to complete the indenture contract, those immigrants who had not brought their families often returned to India to see them again. Goordyal reported that he and his band were offered more money to stay on but could not pass up the opportunity to visit relatives: "We were offered higher wages, even double, when our five years were out, but we wanted to see our children ... My house is at Arrah. I am a Dosaud by caste. I have not sent anything to my family all this time – I have about 150 rupees with me".

Some migrants were helped to return to India by their employers, either sent as recruiters, or assisted to obtain a free passage. Jhurry was a Bihari immigrant from Arrah who went on to become a recruiter of his own countrymen for his Mauritian employers. In 1861 he returned to Calcutta, and described his experiences and plans thus:

> *I was 10 years at Mauritius. My masters were Hart and Bissy, of Grand Port district. As they were very kind to me, I came back to recruit Coolies for them. I have 6 men with me now, who are disposed to accompany me. They come from Arrah Zillah. .... We were well treated on our way from Mauritius. I arrived in the 'Adelaide' 2 months ago.*

In 1873 Rochecouste wrote to the Protector of Immigrants asking for a free passage for Heeraloll and his wife Tarbutty. The couple had been in Mauritius for 25 years and had always resided on his estate at Riche en Eau. Heeraloll had made one trip to India 17 years earlier to recruit labourers. About 5 years past, however, he had become afflicted by leprosy and Heeraloll wanted to return home to see if he could be cured in India. Rochecouste described Heeraloll as "un fort bon homme" who, even after his illness had been kept at gentle labour "dans le but de lui continuer ses gages comme sirdar". Relations between employers and labourers, as this vignette demonstrates, were not necessarily bitter. Men like Heeraloll who were loyal and hard working could expect promotion to a sirdarship and to be looked after by their employers.

Heeraloll, afflicted with leprosy, may not have found the return passage easy. With no interest in delivering healthy passengers - unlike the outbound journey - ship's captains frequently neglected those Indians returning home. Lall Sick, back in India after 7 years away, was highly critical of his treatment on the voyage home in 1844:

> *I served as a labourer and received five Rupees a month and as much as I could eat and was well pleased with the Mauritius and left it having saved about 320 Rs. When we first left Mauritius*

> *we got 24 buckets of water given for our use ... afterwards the number of buckets was reduced to 16, and several men jumped overboard not from ill treatment but from delirium. We complained once to the Captain who said 'if the wind fails, and you drank off the water now what shall we do? If you content yourself with a little you will see your father and mother'.*

As the testimony of Lall Sick indicates, not all Biharis survived the return passage. It was a cruel irony to have gone to Mauritius to earn some money, and after struggling for years, to be deprived of the pleasure of seeing long-lost relatives at the moment of bringing the hard won savings home. Muddanee Sing, a Chatry from Chuprah, died on the return passage in 1845. He was carrying 75 rupees in savings.

Even for those Hindus who returned home safely, there was one final hurdle. Having crossed the *kala pani*, they were required to undertake a purification ceremony. Nankho, who was interviewed by George Grierson at Baksar in 1883, reported that he had acquired most of his money driving a coach in Mauritius, and that on arriving home, he had got married and back into caste at a cost of 100 rupees. With his savings, he had been able to open a shop in his local bazaar.

Some of those who returned with savings were not so prudent. In Shahabad, Grierson spoke to Jibodh, a man of Chamar caste, who was in the process of re-emigrating to Mauritius with his family. After spending 18 years on the island, Jibodh had returned to Bihar with 300 rupees in savings. However, he had lent all his money to friends, interest-free, and after 5 years, realising that he had no income left, had decided to return to the colony. This was not an isolated case - returning migrants were frequently robbed and tricked out of their savings, or were simply too generous with their earnings. It was not easy for those used to a lifetime of poverty, to adjust to new found wealth.

I am beyond supply and demand
Never between the wound and the wand.
I'll shed the insult of low wages,
saviour of the sugar lineages.
Who named the colony after our blood?
The soil was left empty, to dread
our return to the lost country of History.

Chair corail, fragments coolies

The Bihari Muslim Sepoy who became a Mauritian Sirdar: Boodhoo Khan's Story

I am a Pathan, and my home is at Gyah; I left my home in the month of July (Assar) about two years ago; I left my home to seek service. I entered into the service of the rajah of Morbough, as a sepahie, for five rupees per month and food; ... I have a brother in the Calcutta militia, named Sheer Khan. I quarrelled with the rajah's commissary about food, and took my discharge; besides, there was no fighting, or I would have remained. I met with a duffadar at Seersa, in the same district of Morbaugh; he took me to Beerbhul; the duffadar told me ... that I should be five days on the voyage, should get there in a small boat (dinghee), and was to serve for six months at Meritch; I thought it was some island about five days' journey. When I arrived in Calcutta I learnt that I should have to go on board a big ship, and that I was to engage for five years ... I did not mind; I am a man, not a woman, and I am Pathan's son; I had given my word. On arrival at the Mauritius we were taken to the police. We then went to our master, Monsieur Lachiche, whose plantation is at Mappoo, about eight coss north of the city. I remained seven months in my situation of Sirdar ... at the eighth month I was degraded from my sirdarship, and it was given to a Khalashee of the name of Buxoo, who understood French. I was desired to do Coolie work; I refused, and was put in the stocks, I ran away to the police sahib, who saw the marks of the stocks, after which I was desired to do carpenter's work; I said "Give me a musket and I will stand sentry; but I do not know carpenter's work." Upon this I was beaten and again put into the stocks; I broke the stocks and again ran to the police; I was again sent back; and after being beaten, stocked and confined, I tried my hand at carpenter's work.... Mauritius is a good country (howa panee utcha), and the Coolies are all contented; I should not like to return, - why should I? I went as a sirdar, was degraded and put in the stocks, and have left the country - why should I return?

Boodhoo Khan's account of his life before migrating to Mauritius, and his experiences there, as told before the Calcutta Commission of Enquiry in 1838, are so rich in detail, that his story provides a real insight into the men, women and children who are the ancestors of all those in Mauritius today who can trace their lineage back to Bihar. As one of the very earliest indentured migrants to Mauritius, it is doubly fitting to give Boodhoo Khan the last word in this account of their lives.

Sources and Guide for Further Reading

The migrant statements which provided the basis for this study are found in the Parliamentary Papers, and correspondence series in the Indian and British archives. The author's *Voices from Indenture*, Leicester University Press, 1996, provides further details of migrant depositions used for the study of indenture in Mauritius.

Returning from the Sugar Plantation at Dusk

Their shoulders bent forever
under weary loads
Slow they move
As long as they have life.

Tagore

The Recreation of Tradition: Marriage and the Family under Indenture

M. Carter & V. Govinden

Many of the Biharis who came to Mauritius had already experienced seasonal migration for work within India itself. Initially most viewed the overseas indenture contract as simply an extension of such short-term arrangements, and left families at home. The distance to the colony, however, and the length of the term of industrial residence (initially a return passage was granted after five years – this was later extended to ten years) persuaded numbers of immigrants to call for family members to join them. Others returned home as soon as an opportunity arose and collected their kin-folk themselves, taking advantage of bonuses available to men who brought their wives, and elevation to sirdarships for those who recruited fellow-villagers. With the family abroad, the eventual return to Bihar often faded as a dream, with more emphasis placed on the acquisition of land and property in the colony. The Bihari family experienced a period of instability as the pressures of estate labour, the disparity in numbers of women, and the loss of control as parents and spouses in the colonial setting, threatened customary ways of life. Ultimately, however, the Bihari settlers successfully recreated and adapted traditional ceremonies and formalities for their marriages overseas and for the protection of their families.

Migrating Families

Female and family emigration was one aspect of the indenture system which British policy-makers took steps to encourage, and where introduced reforms yielded rapid results. Many of the indentured labourers had viewed migration merely as a temporary device, hoping one day to return to their villages. Those who had left their homes with their families were more inclined to view the migration as a permanent break with the past. The indenture system also created a few 'depot families', hastily formed in the large cities at the behest of the recruiter to avoid costly, time consuming investigation into the background of unattached females by unsympathetic registration officials.

The Mauritian Government realised the benefits of family immigration early on, and introduced a series of measures to raise the number of women and children recruited. It was suggested, for example, *"that natives of India should have ... the grant of a Bonus when they arrive with their own families and others from the same village; [ensuring] in this manner regular settlers and a great saving to the community"*.

Subsequently, pressure on the colonies to increase the proportion of female immigrants came from the Colonial Office. In 1855 Lord John Russell addressed a circular despatch to Mauritius and the West Indies in which he emphasized the intention of Her Majesty's Government to stop Indian emigration unless a due proportion of women was recruited. The introduction of government regulations forbidding the departure of ships without a due percentage of women (usually between 25% to 40% the number of male migrants), produced the desired result. In the early years, prior to the introduction of these rules few women were recruited as labourers. Before 1843 women represented less than 5% of the total immigrant population. This low figure was not surprising as the planters wanted able-bodied men to till the soil, and had specifically instructed their agents to recruit men rather than women. By the mid 19th century, the proportion of women arriving in Mauritius with indentured labourers regularly exceeded 40% and 50% of the male intake. The British authorities continued to support bonuses and incentives for female and family migration because statistics increasingly revealed that disputes over women were the main cause of the high rates of murders and suicides amongst the overseas indentured male population.

In the early years of indenture, as with male immigration, it was tribal women who were once again the pioneers. In 1845, Mr. Caird, the Emigration Agent at Calcutta, remarked that "the majority of the women who have emigrated this year are of the Dhangur caste and likely to be found of the greatest use upon the plantations, being capable of performing any quantity of work". As more indentured labourers returned from Mauritius, others summoned up the courage to take wives and families with them, and all strata of Bihar society began to be represented on the migrant ships: Muslims, high caste and low caste Hindus. Over time, even extended families migrated – aunts, uncles, grandparents, and in-laws were all recensed in the island's immigration register. These family groups, along with single women escaping the stigma of widowhood or poverty in various guises, ensured that the gender imbalance of the Indian population in Mauritius became progressively less marked.

Family Regroupment of Bihari Immigrants

Whilst many men initially made the journey to Mauritius alone, once settled on an estate, or after having moved away from the plantation to establish themselves in villages, they would often call for their families to join them. The contact might be made by letter: writers quickly established themselves amongst the immigrant community, and would draft a missive in the appropriate vernacular for a fee, or through the medium of returning migrants of the same village, who would seek out relatives and pass on messages. Unfortunately, rival recruiters would sometimes lure family members away to the depots of other colonies, so that the best laid plans of migrants in Mauritius to be rejoined by their families could go awry.

If family members succeeded in passing the medical examination required of all recruits, and arriving in the right colony, they would be indentured to a plantation which was seeking labour at that time, rather than to the estate on which their relatives were already residing. To prevent kin being sent to a distant estate, immigrants already in Mauritius devised a means of obtaining information as to when family members had arrived, and then intervening before they were engaged elsewhere. Women were usually allowed to go if a male relative claimed them, but newly arrived male immigrants had to be bought out of indenture. When Ramotar learnt that his brother, Puguth, had arrived from Arrah, and was at the depot, he addressed the following letter to the Protector of Immigrants:

31st March 1884
Poudre d'Or
Sir,
Having heard that my brother has come to Mauritius as a Coolee, I have most respectfully come to see you about his delivery. He is the only brother I have, and I have not seen him for upwards of thirty years. I have a great desire to take him with me;
I have therefore most humbly come to see you and beg to inform you that I will pay for his delivery, what a proprietor will pay to take him. I earnestly beg you to let me have him instead of a proprietor for he is the only brother I have.
The following will be his description -
Name – Puguth, Father's name – Soohumber, Mother's name – Goora, Native country - Arrah.

Hoping Sir, that you will accord me my demand I have the honor to be Sir, your most obedient humble servant,
Ramotar.

The arrival of immigrant women was equally a great source of interest to single men, and if it became known that a group of single women were in the depot, the Protector would receive a flood of letters from individuals hoping to find a spouse. Kurmally, also of Arrah, gave as his reason for requiring a wife from the depot the "impossibility of getting my breakfast cooked in the morning on account of the distance sometimes I have to work, and to take care of my orphan children". When Boodhun saw an attractive woman, Keseerah, at the depot, he decided to inform the Protector that they were already married! The Protector subsequently minuted "This man acknowledged that the women was not his wife, but that she came from the same part of India, and he would like to have her". Of course women had the option to refuse the suitors who presented themselves, but in practice, overseas migration offered many young widows the opportunity to remarry which was denied them in India.

'Sisterhood'

Marriages in Mauritius

To validate marriages transacted in India, where civil registration was not the norm, arriving couples were issued with a marriage certificate. However, it was difficult to give this force of law, and until an Indian Marriage Ordinance was framed, male immigrants found that they had no legal redress if their wives were inveigled away. Thus, even when the marriage was valid according to Indian ritual and custom, with the couple arriving together as man and wife, the union was subject to the pressures of life on the estate camps, where sirdars and planters posed a formidable threat to a man's control over his wife. The penal clauses of the estate contract, which resulted in absentee and even sick labourers receiving prison sentences, could be used to savage effect by employers and overseers wanting to separate a man from his wife. Many of the immigrants deliberately left their wives behind knowing that a married woman was vulnerable in the colonies.

As the Indian population increased in size over the course of the 19th century, the British administration began to express concerns about the paucity of civil marriages and the inability of the government to regulate age at marriage amongst the immigrant community:

> *A very large number of Indian couples in Mauritius are living together without any Civil Marriage having been performed. Most of them have been married according to their own religion and customs but others have not been married at all and are simply living together in concubinage. Marriages among Indians, whether contracted legally or according to their own rites and customs, always cost money in clothing, and feasting. Hence the reason why so many live together as man and wife ... and postpone the religious or civil marriage to a more prosperous time.*
>
> *... Indian marriages are usually contracted at a very early age; it is true that husband and wife do not live together till the girl has attained the age of puberty, say 12 or 13 years, but the*

> *marriages take place when the children are very young and in most instances long before the girl is 15 years of age. In India children are frequently married to elderly men when the latter are possessed of property or money and similar marriages have taken place in this colony.*
>
> *According to the law of this colony the marriageable age for men and women is fixed at 18 and 15 respectively and this is one of the reasons why there are so many illegal marriages as most Indian girls are married according to their own religion and personal law before they attain the age of 15 years.*
>
> *Once the religious marriage has taken place very few Indians care about legalizing their marriage under the civil law and as a rule it is only when they become possessed of property that they have recourse to civil marriage wishing thereby to secure their property to their children.*

Even those Biharis who did opt for a civil marriage might find difficulties thrown in their way. Sunghoreea, a woman of the Dosaud caste from Arrah, protested to the Protector that the Civil Status officer at Pamplemousses refused to celebrate the marriage of her daughter. It emerged that the girl's father had not given his consent to it, but since he had disappeared 14 years earlier, it was not likely that this could be obtained. The man concerned, Dulsinger, had in fact come to Mauritius with two wives who were both listed as his spouses on his immigration certificate. All three were from the same village, and the other wife, Rujkoleea, was 3 years younger than her co-wife, arriving at the age of 17 with the 20 year old Sunjhoreea and their shared husband. The daughter of the latter also came with the group. She was aged two and a half at the time of their arrival in 1858.

Immigrants like Dulsinger's daughter who arrived in Mauritius as children, were among the first generation to marry in the colony itself. If they were from a region that was poorly represented on the island, or from a small sub-caste, they had no other option than to contract exogamous marriages. In such circumstances, preference was usually given to a partner from the same linguistic group and a nearby region. The large caste groups such as Ahir, Kurmi, Koeri, Kahar, Gowalla and Chamar Biharis, however, were generally able to find spouses from within their caste. High caste Rajputs and Bramins also tended to intermarry, thereby retaining their separate status.

With the re-establishment of acceptable partner selection in the new setting, came the ceremonies and the expenses of contracting and organising a wedding. Male immigrants who undertook the cost of a traditional marriage, were deeply aggrieved if their wives subsequently left the conjugal roof. Not always able to afford or to obtain justice in the courts, they turned to the Protector to intercede on their behalf. In 1881, Jowankul, a labourer at "Mon Tresor" in Grand Port, sent in a complaint about his wife Behchnye, daughter of Seebaluck and Bataseea of St Marie Estate, Savanne. "The said marriage was in Hindoo rites performed by our priest", he wrote, adding that he had spent in "money and other expenses for the said marriage, about eight hundred rupees". The wife later ran back to her parents "with all my money and jewels". She was then pregnant with his child - a boy - now 5 months old and who was declared by her parents. Jowankul understood that he had no legal rights over his wife "being not regularly married [except] in my religion," but he felt that the parents "married to me their daughter expressly to get my money and took their child back". The Protector could only reply: "inform petitioner that I can do nothing for him and that if his reputed wife has stolen his money he can bring a charge against her for the theft before a magistrate".

When marriages took place between the new elite of the indentured community – the sirdars and small tradesmen – the sums and gifts involved were so costly as to necessitate the drawing up of a legal contract. In 1874 notary Maingard recorded the marriage contract between Ramessur and Soodale. The bridegroom was the son of Sirdar Ramchurn of Pamplemousses. His bride, the daughter of Beeroo, was still a minor. Both had been born in India, and migrated at a very young age with their parents. The contract specified that Soodale was to receive

45 rings or necklaces of silver and gold worth 100 piastres, clothing and other goods worth 50 piastres, 1 cow and 4 goats worth 100 piastres, and a cash sum of 150 piastres. This was a substantial settlement on a girl who was effectively still a child.

Nuptial Song

*Little husband
Pure water bring
from my orchard
dig your desired land
dig my friend*

*In the golden cage
the budgie will sing
The night is ravished
for you
the moon has vanished*

*At Bihar Patna
the veils of the beloved
unravel the veranda,
around you
the flower will caress the canna*

*Garlands I blend
The nail of the moon
I bend*

*The Rice
on the square stone
I spread*

*Exile in a mustard paste
I grind
O little husband
For you I am at Hand*

Chair corail, fragments coolies

Children of Diaspora

During the indenture period, very young children were expected to work on the estates. Children who were little more than toddlers were given simple tasks to perform, whilst those aged 10 and over could be engaged for long periods and expected to perform full time labouring jobs. It thus occurred that teenagers could be indentured to estates and subjected to the same punishments as adult men. In 1873 one employer, Rondeaux of Bel Ombre, took the exceptional step of approaching the Protector to reverse the punishment inflicted on one of his labourers. He explained that in March of the previous year he had attended the Stipendiary Magistrate's court to get several men condemned for illegal absence. Among them was a young Indian, Beekano, who was given 14 days imprisonment. As Rondeaux explained in his letter to the Protector:

> *Il parait que cette condemnation equivaut pour un jeune Indien à deux ans de Penitencier. La mère de cet Indien, porteur de la présente, étant attristéee de l'éloignement prolongé de son fils Beekano m'a supplié de le faire libérer. J'ai fait à cet effet plusieurs vaines démarches auprès de Messrs Daly et Fleming et je prends la liberté de venir aujourd'hui m'adresser à vous dans l'espoir que vous pourrez faire mettre en liberté le jeune Indien.*

The Protector, investigating the case, noted that the boy's mother, Beejmee, was a widow, having only her son Beekano, and a 16 year old daughter. He subsequently addressed a letter to the Stipendiary Magistrate, on the subject.

Parents could thus find that the colonial state's tendency to treat children as responsible adults brought severe punishments when youngsters ran away from harsh employers or misbehaved at the workplace. Bihari and other immigrant children found wandering the streets were regularly condemned before a Magistrate to incarceration for a period of several years in the juvenile reformatory. Parents were forced to plead - often in vain - for the return of their children. In 1883, the Protector was able to inform two Bihari fathers, Joypaul, a labourer of Beau Champ, and Budreesingh of La Providence, Flacq, that the Governor had agreed with his recommendation, and remitted the remainder of the sentence of their sons. Seleckram, Ramsanahee, and Seegolam, all held at the reformatory, were free to go home to their anxious parents.

Beekano, the young indentured labourer whose mother persuaded his employer to secure his release from prison

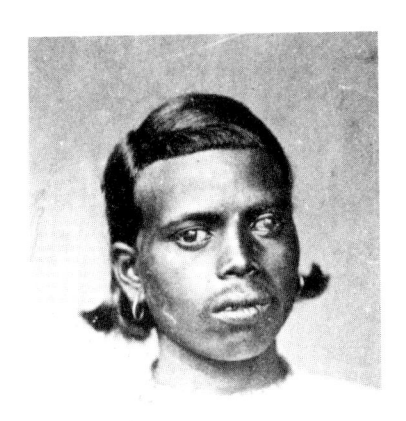

When immigrant parents died, relatives or friends of the deceased would take charge of the orphans. In 1881, Suggoona, the Marathi wife of a Bihari immigrant, Ragu, "a herder in goats and cows", sought to adopt a child whose parents had died in Barkly Asylum and who were friends of theirs. Whilst such de facto adoptions obviated the need to place children in the strict government-run orphanage, it also meant that parentless children were prey to unscrupulous adults, who aimed to benefit financially from putting the orphans out to work.

When two girls, Boodeea and Ramkaleea, were orphaned by the death of their parents on the same day in an accident at Pointe aux Piments, relatives fought to obtain custody of them and their affairs. Ramkalia, who was 14 years of age, was married off to Paraboo's son, and the father-in-law sought to to be appointed their guardian. Their grandmother, a Bihari woman named Khedeeah, declared for her part that she wished to have the care of her grand daughter Boodheea. The police list of the belongings of the girls' parents, including silver ornaments, clothes, furniture and cows and an acre of land planted with sugar canes, help to explain the competing claims for guardianship.

Few Bihari immigrants left a will or even used a bank to keep their hard earned savings. When a labourer died, those who knew where the pot of coins was buried, could simply dig it up. For those labourers who had amassed some property, and had placed their wealth in safe hands, the Curator of Vacant Estates would oversee the sale of any land and valuables, and would decide the rights of family in Mauritius to inherit the proceeds together with any wages due. Children's interests were safeguarded by the Protector, who was himself the guardian of Indian orphans. When Seebnauth died on Highlands estate leaving a bank deposit book, several *bons* of some value and a natural son called Ramdass Seebnauth born in 1881, the Protector's first concern was for the boy. He noted that the mother was living with another Indian on the same estate and claimed "it is very probable if the money came into her hands it would be squandered to the prejudice of the minor". In this case the Protector applied to be appointed guardian of Ramdass "whose interests would be thereby protected", even though the boy still had a living mother.

Fortunately, some migrants were able to do without the interference of colonial officials by organising family councils which could decide on the best means of protecting the rights of minors. These meetings were recorded by notaries and given force of law. In 1867 the Family Council of Sobahsing of Pamplemousses, a proprietor, was convened in the name four minors, acknowledged by him and their late mother

Anjoreea as their natural children, to appoint a guardian for them. The gathering of family and friends provides an insight into the small networks which immigrants were forging to manage their affairs. Sobahsing was supported by Munkurum of Pamplemousses, a baker and his brother in law and Padaruth also of Pamplemousses, a baker, and friend. To represent the mother, Chukun, Taukoor and Bhurtun of Pamplemousses, all cultivators, were convened. The council decided that Sobasing would be the guardian whilst Taukoor would assist him in his duties.

All Busy

In the matter of inheritance rights, as in so much else, Bihari and other Indian immigrants sought to recreate the norms and forms of the society they had left. As labourers realised the benefits of settling on the island, bringing families, or marrying in Mauritius, so they began to acquire property and land on which to establish a return to a semblance of village life. The reinstitution of customary marriage settlements and wedding ceremonies was one of the first symbols of this recreation of Bihari traditions in the new setting.

Sources and Guide for Further Reading

The material for this article was collected at the Mauritius Archives and supplemented with information from the Indian Immigration Archive of the Mahatma Gandhi Institute. A more detailed study of female and family migration to Mauritius can be found in M. Carter, *Lakshmi's Legacy*, EOI, 1994.

The Making of a New Community: Socio-Economic Change and the Bihari Hindus

M.Carter, S. Deerpalsingh & V. Govinden

The cultural landscape of Mauritius was irrevocably altered by the arrival of thousands of Bihari labourers over the course of the 19th century. Small temples appeared in the countryside, and a new class of small planters and market gardeners was created. The socio-cultural associations which emerged from the years of indenture laid the foundations for the political organisations which ultimately brought Biharis to the forefront of the island's governing institutions. New horizons had opened for the indentured labourers within a few decades of their arrival which few could have imagined on first disembarking at the Aapravasi Ghat.

Avenues of Economic Success: Sirdars and Landowners

One of the earliest means of achieving economic mobility was for Bihari immigrants to capitalise on the opportunities available in the management and recruitment of other indentured labourers. Sirdarships were up for grabs from the moment the first bands of ' coolies' stood on the wharf at Port Louis. Men who appeared to have an air of authority, or maturity, were plucked from their fellow labourers and appointed to one of these crucial intermediary roles between the planter and his work-force. A sirdar was expected to supervise the work of his men, to round up absentees and to control teams working on set tasks. His role was ambiguous – the sirdar was expected to stand up for the men in his band whilst carrying out the orders of his employer. Those sirdars who defied authority and led their men in complaints, could find themselves demoted and ruined. Above all, the sirdar enjoyed a higher wage than the average labourer and the potential to make more. His income could be supplemented from recruiting activities, either in Mauritius or through trips to India, and moneylending.

Such men, the first natural leaders of the Bihari community in Mauritius, were surprisingly mobile. Nanoo Parry, who arrived in the colony on 23 June 1854, had made several trips to and from India by 1865, when he again returned as a free passenger. He was a Brahmin from Arrah.

It was not unusual for labourers to entrust the sirdar with their wages. In 1858 the Chief Sirdar of Industrie estate had so much ready cash that he was in a position to lend money to his own employer. When the Stipendiary Magistrate of Pamplemousses ruled against Mr F Pellegrin, proprietor of l'Industrie, for wages due to his engaged men, the chief sirdar lent him the sum of £370. Pellegrin promised to pay it back within 8 days. In 1870 the sirdar was still waiting for the return of his loan. He engaged Mr Felix, an Attorney, to prosecute his claim but in vain, and was consequently unable to return the money to his band, who wished to take their savings home. He resorted to asking the Protector, "as our self-defender to prescribe me the way for obtaining the same sum which we have spared from the hardest labour of 22 years in this colony".

The capital that accrued to this new elite of the indenture system did not all flow out of the colony through returning migrants. Many of the more successful sirdars purchased land in Mauritius and went into sugar cane cultivation or market gardening on their own account. They were assisted in this by the crisis of the sugar industry in the 1860s and the resulting *morcellements*, or parcelling up of marginal lands on the peripheries of the large estates. Some labourers acquired land through employers defaulting on wage payments. This was how Sunkur, a Kurmi from Arrah, and fellow labourers Tankoor, Rampul and Jobalsing, became the joint owners of a ten acre plot of ground at Le Pont Praslin in Pamplemousses around 1865.

Having acquired land, the Biharis looked for suitable and lucrative business opportunities. Goorachand Lala and Seewoodharree Buguth became substantial employers when they went into the charcoal business. In 1873 they were described as "the proprietors of extensive forest lands at Vacoas and employ some hundreds of Indians as wood cutters and charcoal burners". The large scale of their operation provoked suspicion from the police who believed that they might be acting as a 'cloak for vagabondage'. The authorities compromised by requiring the men to take out licences. Seewoodharry Buguth was a man of many guises, a useful attribute for an Indian entrepreneur. He also made a living from job contracting, a system under which the planter paid a fixed fee to the contractor to harvest his canes, rather than employing cutters directly.

Most of the Biharis who saved money through a combination of sirdarships, job contracting, recruiting or simple hard labour, contented themselves with the acquisition of a few arpents of land on which to establish a small plantation or a vegetable patch. A few had grander ambitions. Ramtohul, a Rajput from Patna, who arrived in Mauritius in 1856 as a 34 year old indentured immigrant, had managed to buy his own sugar estate in 1870. Sadly, the new owner of Mon Choix estate did not have long to enjoy his new found status, dying the following year.

The Restructuring of Religion

On the estates, Indians built small temples dedicated to Shiva, where other deities such as Sita, Durga, and Vishnu were also worshipped. Ram and Hanuman were particular favourites of the Biharis, and a small stone dedicated to Hanuman with a lamp lit by it, was a feature of many camps. Pujas were also organised, with donations being solicited for events such as the Bahariya Puja, where a goat would be sacrificed. Those sirdars who were also Bramins, could supplement their earnings by capitalising on the priestly functions of their caste. When the Bihari Bramin, Bonomally, a sirdar on Alma Estate at Moka, died in 1884, his Attorny, Arthur Pitot, informed the Protector, "the deceased having been a priest I am informed that it is absolutely necessary that a costly ceremony be celebrated at a fixed date after his death". Those wealthy sirdars and landowners of the Bihari community who were not priests themselves played a part in the implantation of their religion in Mauritius through donations of land and money for the construction of temples.

This manuscript of the Ramayana in 'kaithi' script was brought to Mauritius by an Indian Immigrant in 1842

There are no headstones, epitaphs, dates.
The ancestors curl and dry to scrolls of parchment.
They lie like texts
Waiting to be written by the children
For whom they hacked and ploughed and saved
To send to faraway schools.

David Dabydeen

(i) The Organisation of Temple Construction

Visiting Mauritius in 1860, Alfred Erny noticed at Plaine Lauzun on the outskirts of Port Louis, "un pittoresque temple" which was a miniature version of the famous Temple of Juggernauth in India. A decade later the Royal Commissioners and Estate Inspectors reported seeing several makeshift temples and religious classes in progress on the estates. The 1858 petition of 'a Hindoo religious mendicant' Govindgaree, praying for a piece of land on which to build a temple at Grande Riviere, sparked off a wider debate about the desirability and placement of Indian villages, as the British authorities belatedly recognised that the location of centres of worship would prove a pole of attraction for the Hindu and Muslim labourers. The first Hindu temples were constructed through means of donations collected chiefly from the ordinary labourers. By the end of the 19th century, a small group of individuals, priests and sirdars among them, had emerged as the leaders of the religious revival of Hinduism in Mauritius.

Not all of the early attempts at cooperation for the establishment of temple funds were successful. In 1872, Seetohul wrote to the Protector, explaining that his "countrymen of Hindu creed have charged him to collect money to build a church … Since five years your petitioner has been from place to place collecting money for the erection of that church and for the ceremonies of religion according to the Hindu creed". During this time Seetohul collected 250 dollars. Unfortunately, the money was entrusted to Ramhit alias Ramlugun, who acted as their treasurer, and who subsequently absconded to India with the funds.

In 1880, a plan of local Hindus to construct a temple at Pamplemousses, was better organised, and those involved included significant leaders of their co-religionists. Aware that Indians in Mauritius were becoming mistrustful of individuals purportedly collecting 'temple funds', the new project provided for better guarantees. In July 1880 Seepalsing and Gunness Geetu accordingly requested the Protector to take care of the funds himself:

That your petitioners together with other immigrants of their creed are desirous of erecting a church in the district of Pamplemousses. That in order of carrying out their intention they have purchased a plot of ground in the said district from one Jean Peguillau, in virtue of a notarial deed of Mr Planel, a notary, dated the 24th of November last.

That in order that the said church should be erected, funds must be collected, by way of contribution, from other Indians belonging to the same creed.

That your Petitioners and others of their fellow countrymen have been appointed to collect the said funds in the said district and also in other districts of the said colony.

That in consequence of a certain distrust prevailing to the effect that the trustees might apply the said funds to other purposes than those for which they were destined, they have not succeeded in their mandate.

Your Petitioners are aware that attempts at erecting churches in other districts have not succeeded, Indians being unwilling to hand over their money, for the above mentioned purposes, to men of their own nationality.

Your petitioners respectfully hope that your honor, as Protector of Immigrants, would condescend to receive, for the account of the church at Pamplemousses, whatever money should be handed over to you by your Petitioners, and also by trustees appointed as above explained, which money should be returned by you to the said trustees in proportion to the requirements of the church to be built, only upon receipts signed by the said trustees.

And your Petitioners feeling confident that your honor will kindly accede to this your Petitioners' request, will ever pray as in duty bound.

Pamplemousses, twentieth day of July 1880

The Protector's reply of 27 July 1880 suggested that the petitioners should "choose four or six persons in whose name all your subscriptions may be deposited in the Savings Bank - and the book left with the cashier of this office, on the understanding that no money shall be withdrawn unless all the depositors or a certain number of them join in asking to take money out".

By October 1881, a new spokesman for the project, Dhumun Napaul, was in correspondence with the Protector. A resident of Montagne Longue, Napaul reported that he had just returned from India where he had consulted temple designers: "ce voyage a été dans le but de chercher différents plans de pagodes indiens". Having obtained permission for its construction, Dhumun wished to add his name to the list of the 'trustees' already deposited with the Protector, "afin de jouir en même temps du privilège de ses amis". He also requested permission to place an advertisement in the newspaper so that his fellow Indians would be made aware of the plans, and could be invited to subscribe. The list of names of the directors of the temple project was as follows: Seepalsing, Gunness Geer, Dhumun, Abeeluck Maraz, Beecome Maraz, and Ajoodhusing.

By the last decades of the 19th century, the Hindu religion was flourishing in many forms and across all districts. In Triolet, Sanjibonlall Ramsoondur had gifted to the Hindu Society of the locality, a portion of land measuring 10 arpents together with the temple constructed upon it and all dependent buildings. The private benefactors of the indenture years were giving way before a new era of organised religious associations. Accepting the donation on behalf of the society were a group of respectable members of the Hindu community from diverse regions of the colony. They included Bhusunt, son of sirdar Jhuboo, Nundoosing, son of sirdar Hungsraz of Moka, Dabysing and Gungadinsing of Grand Port, Napal of Flacq, Nunkeesoon and Mohabeersingh of Port Louis, Gujadhur of Plaines Wilhems, Ramjane Sing of Riviere des Anguilles, Chakoor of Rose Hill, Boodhun Lallah of Curepipe, Ramparsad Naridoo of Riviere Noire, Rampersad Pudaruth of Vacoas and others from Plaines Wilhems and Pamplemousses.

(ii) The Origins of the Pilgrimage to 'Ganga Talao'

If the Hindu Society represented Indians of various regional and caste groupings, the flurry of temple building and the increasing recognition of religious leaders inevitably brought divisions and disputes. Competition between priests officiating at Grand Bassin at the turn of the century is one example of this.

The institution of an annual pilgrimage to this upland lake is usually credited to an ex-indentured labourer from Arrah, Jhumun Seesahye, who reportedly dreamt in 1897 of the holy Ganges water springing from it. Through this 'dream', Jhumun was able to transplant traditional forms of worship at the banks of the Ganges in India to Grand Bassin in Mauritius. The occasion of Maha Shivaratri thus began to be celebrated with an annual pilgrimage to the lake.

In fact the available documents suggest that a temple, or shrine, had been built at Grand Bassin, and that pilgrimages had taken place well before that date, on 1st and 2nd January of each year, in accordance with the New Year holiday. In fact, in 1895, the temple was already the subject of a dispute between Jhumun, now established as a priest at Moka, and a rival, Teeluckdharry, resident in Savanne. Jhumun had arrived from Bihar as a 14 year old in January 1860 and was engaged to the estate of Bon Accueil. His caste was listed as 'Gosye'. He went to India in 1880, returning in August 1881 when his occupation was recorded as that of shopkeeper. Both priests claimed to be the owner of the *ashthan*, and, according to the Protector of Immigrants who sought to resolve the dispute:

> *Teeluckdharry is a brahmin and Jhummun Seesahye a Gosain, so that their religious services should not be performed at one and the same shrine.... This temple at Grand Bassin has existed for many years and large numbers of Hindoos make a pilgrimage to it every year, so that the place is now looked upon by them*

with a certain amount of veneration, much in the same manner as they regard the Ganges in India as a sacred river.

It was decided that Seesahye should be allowed to construct a second temple "at about 20 paces from the one now in existence". In a private conversation with the Protector, Jhumun explained the finer points of the theological differences which separated his congregation from Teeluckdharry's followers, and these were summarised by the Protector as follows:

The other lot are Brahmins, Jhumun Seesahaye's lot are Gosains. Jhumun is a worshipper of Mahadeo. The others worship Vishnu and Brahma. Jhummun says that he does not go in for the sacrifice of cocks and the others do.

It was also agreed that Jhumun could cover his shrine with an iron roof. In the event, however, the Director of Forests and Gardens refused to allow the roof to be placed on the temple. By the end of 1896, with his temple completed, Jhumun again contacted the Protector who supported his request on the grounds that "it is generally very wet during the first few days of each year when annual pilgrimages are made to Grand Bassin and it would consequently be a great boon not only to the priests but to the pilgrims if they could obtain temporary shelter under the iron roof of the temple." The Governor refused to allow the roof because "permission was only given him to build an altar similar to the one about 20 feet distant, and which has no roof or covering".

Jhumun had evidently not resolved the dispute with Teeluckdharry to his satisfaction, for a year later, in January 1898, he presented another proposal for the consideration of the Protector. His petition read:

Nouvelle Decouverte, Moka, le 12 Janvier 1898
A L'Honorable Protecteur des Immigrants

L'humble petition de Joomun Seesaye, pretre Hindoo, demeurant a la Nouvelle Decouverte, district de Moka, pres de la Gare St Pierre, soumet respectueusement a Votre Honneur la presente.
Que votre petitionnaire avait ete autorise en 1896 par Son Excellence, a construire un temple Hindoo a Grand Bassin pres de celui d'un autre pretre Hindoo nomme Teeluckdharry.
Que n'ayant pas pu etre d'accord avec Teeluckdharry, votre petitionnaire n'a point construit de temple.
Votre petitionnaire a trouve un endroit convenable a eriger un temple c'est a la Riviere des Lataniers dans un endroit planté ou il existe beaucoup d'arbres, mais l'endroit qu'il a choisi n'a pas d'arbre plante dessus, aussi a t'il l'intention d'en planter apres l'erection du temple afin d'embellir l'endroit.
Votre petitionnaire vient respectueusement vous prier de le faire obtenir cet endroit.

The Bihari Priest, Jhumun Seesahye

Seesahye also informed the Protector that if the land could not be given to him he would be glad to know if he could buy it and what the price would be. He was willing to point out the spot to the Director of Woods and Forests. However, he once again met a refusal. The Colonial Secretary replied that "the land pointed out by [Jhumun] to Mr Hily at Abercrombie, is covered with Eucalyptus, Bois noir and Campeachy trees".

In the meantime the Grand Bassin dispute continued. In June 1899 the Protector described the position again: "they are two Indian priests, each of whom has a large following of hindoos. An ill feeling has existed between them for many years as each thinks the other reduces the number of his followers. Their gala time is the 1st and 2nd January of each year when they scoop in all the money they can from the hindoos who believe in them at Grand Bassin, where each has a small temple. This lake is now regarded by them as more or less sacred". Their animosity was also personal – Jhumun had given evidence against Teeluckdharry in a case brought against him for stealing some dry wood from Government premises. Seesahye offered Teeluckdharry Rs 24 a year provided he would agree not to hold any more services at his temple at Grand Bassin.

Moreover, as the popularity of the lake as a site of pilgrimage grew, other priests requested to be allowed to officiate at Grand Bassin. As the end of 1899 Ramroche, a Hindu priest living at Midlands was informed that "no special authority is necessary to celebrate ceremonies according to Hindoo religious rites at Grand Bassin during the first two or three days of the new year. All that it is necessary for him to do is to avoid interfering with two Hindoo priests named Teeluckdharry and Jhumun Seesahye, each of whom has a small platform on which he performs his religious ceremonies".

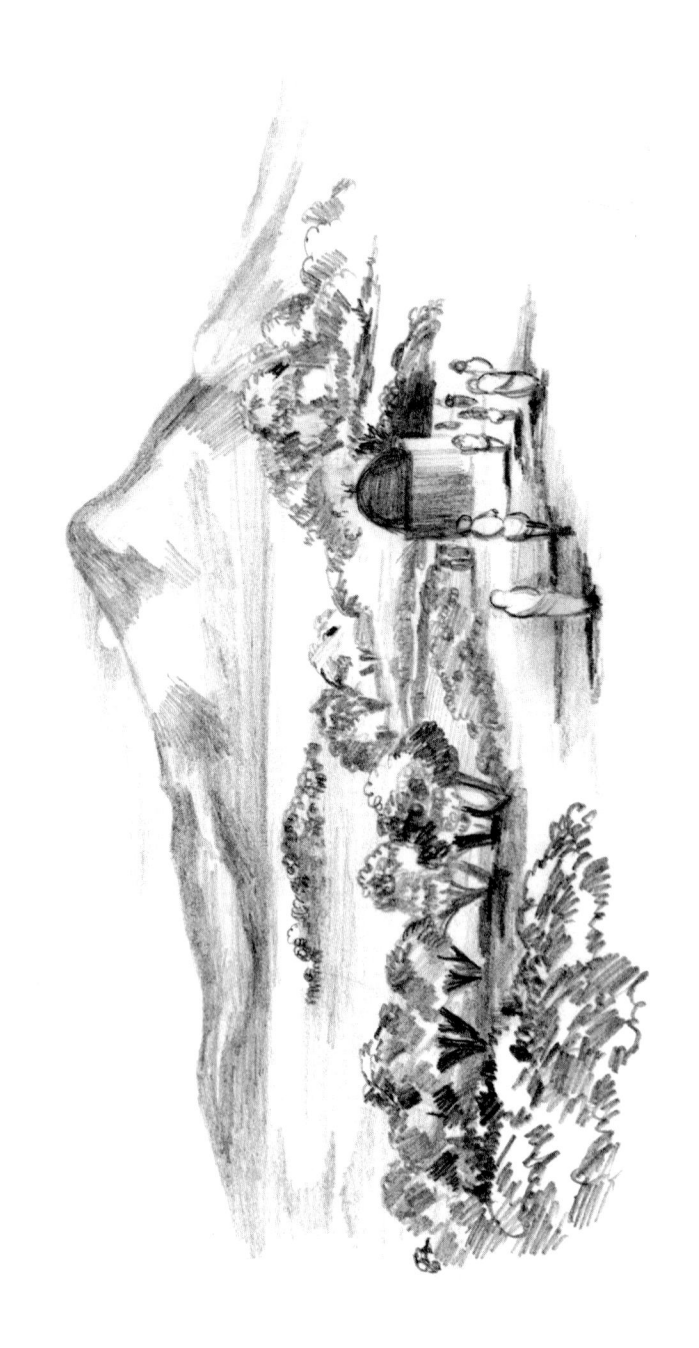

A View of Grand Bassin in the 19th Century

Pilgrims Converging on Grand Bassin

The beleaguered Seesahye subsequently complained about the activities of a fourth priest. In January 1900 he addressed yet another petition to the Governor, which was summarised by the Protector as follows: "what Jhumun Seesahye complains of now is that another hindoo priest named Emraz pitched his hut either on or near his temple at Grand Bassin during the first 2 or 3 days of this year and prevented him from carrying on his religious functions at Grand Bassin and that Emraz was incited to do this by his old enemy Teeluckdharry". The Protector interviewed Emraz and was informed that the priest had officiated at a spot close to Seesahye's temple and had as a result quarreled with both him and Teeluckdharry. The Governor sought to draw the correspondence to a close by informing the petitioner that he could not "interfere in quarrels that take place between him and other hindoo priests at the Grand Bassin". Jhumun died in 1914, and despite the early disputes between those who sought to lead the faithful in prayers, the importance of what would become 'Ganga Talao' far outweighed the individual personalities who had begun the pilgrimage.

The Recreation of Village Life

As Bihari and other Indian immigrants began to move off the plantations into settlements created through *morcellements* and other forms of land acquisition, the need to re-establish village-level organisations became apparent. Whilst some disputes could be resolved by approaching the Protector or petitioning the Governor, establishing the identity of competing legatees, or proving the status of married couples and other family members could often only be ascertained by collecting together a group of one's respectable neighbours who could vouch for one party or the other. Thus when Bahooram, of Terrain Fouquereaux, Phoenix, attempted to demonstrate in 1874 that his savings of $295 had been stolen and spent by his wife Alhajee Goodory in company with a man named Lutchmansing, he took steps to put his case in a traditional manner. As he stated:

I have gathered some Indians of high character and formed a council to take these sayings into consideration and these are the names of the persons who were present: Soondursing - entrepreneur; Pyroo - gardener; Sirdharsun - Sirdar of Highlands estate; Sajeewon - gardener; Babooa - gardener, Ramsahaye - gardener, Paravay - shopkeeper; Beeharry - Sirdar of Highlands estate; Cheekoorally - a small proprietor; Sidhaivon - shopkeeper; Babransing - Sirdar of Highlands estate; Bhowanee - mercerie vendor. All these persons can certify whether it is true or not.

Such gatherings were the precursors of *panchayati* organisations in Mauritius. As villages became established, *baitkas* were built, so that community organisations could be housed in a specific location. Numerous events, which were in themselves important affirmations of a community and a cultural identity, now centred around the baitka. The traditional spring festival of Holi was held there – when *hawan* offerings were performed and cakes distributed. Verses of the Ramayana would also be sung in the baitka. Through open air stagings of the Ram Lilas, through folk songs, games and traditional wrestling, the culture of the Bihari village was transplanted to the tropical island of Mauritius.

These affirmations of cultural identity and the village-level organisations which were established by Bihari immigrants, were the starting point of the affirmation of an Indian political identity in the early 20th century. The battles of the Hindu scriptures could be transformed into a powerful political message in the hands of a skilled orator. From the economic success of the sirdars and the religious and cultural induction of the baitkas, a new political elite was in the process of formation.

The Afternoon Meeting

I will end the monopoly of the merits of birth
in the land of pillage and scuttle;
Poet I vow:
"For each of us there is space in the conquest
time will appoint ..."

Chair corail, fragments coolies

Sources and Guide for Further Reading

The documentation used in this article was chiefly obtained from the Mauritius Archives and supplemented by data from the Indian Immigration Archive of the Mahatma Gandhi Institute. Sarita Boodhoo's Bhojpuri Traditions in Mauritius, 1999, is a useful guide to the articulation of a regional cultural identity. A.S. Simmons, Modern Mauritius, 1982, covers the political history of the Indians.

Serenity

Socio-Economic Mobility among Bihari Muslims

Amenah Jahangeer-Chojoo

Muslims formed a conspicuous minority among the indentured immigrants from Bihar. Hailing from various social strata but mostly from modest backgrounds they have emerged from indentureship and plantation life with unequal success. While some managed to improve their socio-economic position through the ownership of a plot of land, thus establishing themselves in the small planter class, for many it was through commercial and other activities that they were able to better their lot. Urbanization, changing occupations and education have all been instrumental in the socio-economic progression of Muslim families.

Progress on the economic front has often been accompanied with a greater involvement in socio-religious activities, such as the practice of religious rituals with greater rigour as well as performing benevolent, community-based activities, such as the construction of a mosque, in order to gain recognition and respectability.

Patterns in the socio-economic evolution of Bihari Muslims can be constructed from family histories. The Muslim immigrants originated mostly from the populous districts of Bihar and the eastern United Provinces, though a small minority came from South India and the Bombay Presidency. Owing to the numerical preponderance of the first group the Muslim indentured immigrants are lumped together under the generic term of "*Calcuttyas*", and few regional distinctions have been preserved.

Acquisition of Land

Land ownership was for many ex-indentured labourers the first step towards economic improvement. Small plots of land were available during the *"grand morcellement"* period starting from the 1860s and lasting through to the beginning of the twentieth century, when crises in the sugar industry forced many family plantations to be dismantled.

Mr S...., No. 250 658 who arrived from the zillah of Arrah in 1859 with his wife and son, bought a plot of ½ Arpent of land in Savanne in 1866 from a Miss Lucile Cante. He purchased a second plot of 1 Arpent together with another immigrant in 1875, from a Gujarati commercial firm. Mr S. died in 1877 leaving two sons and a daughter.

Ahmode Dastagheer, who is presumed to be a Calcuttya ex-indentured labourer though we do not have his indentureship number, bought a plot of 1½ Arpents as early as 1852 in Plaines Wilhems from Miss Elizabeth Marie for 80 Piastres but had to sell it three years later. He would buy land again as from 1884, or 29 years later.

In these cases the sellers of plots were either ladies of slave or free origins, or intermediaries, like the Gujarati firm who bought land and parcelled it out. The buyers had paid cash. The sons or grandsons of these immigrants would become large or medium landholders but all of them would pass through other occupations than traditional land cultivation before returning to agriculture. Their itineraries are sketched below.

Alhaman, the son of S., bought small plots of land of less than 1 Arpent as from 1890 often in association with one or several persons. His occupation was declared to be trade. In this way he acquired 22 small plots between 1890 and 1901. In 1901 he bought a large plot of 37 Arpents in Grand Port from a Gujarati firm and two plantations of 136 and 215 Arpents at Savanne from a group of ex-indentured Indian owners, who for their part, had acquired them jointly at a judicial sale. He had now become a large landholder and continued to increase his property, buying small and large plots. By 1907 began to diversify his investments and acquired urban plots in Mahébourg, Curepipe and Port Louis. He went on to buy several large estates before he died in 1928, so becoming one of the richest persons of Indian origin.

The case of Ahmode Dustagheer and his son Abdoula is particularly illustrative of the economic opportunities prevailing at the end of the 19th and beginning of the 20th century. They participated fully in the "*grand morcellement*" by becoming active agents in the parcelling out of land. With the financial support of commercial houses in Port Louis of Gujarati and local origins they managed to participate on a large scale in land transactions of that period and make a fortune, which was quickly lost.

In fact, Ahmode Dustagheer also earned some money and fame through the practise of Indian wrestling as he was a "*Calipa*" (wrestler). Games were held on plantations or in town especially during the "*Tajjia*" festivities. It is supposed that money obtained from this occupation was used to buy small plots of land between 1884 and 1894. In 1894 he and his son Abdoula bought an estate of 222 Arpents in Savane from T.Sauzier and G.Martin. The cost was Rs 40 000, with a down payment of Rs 6 000 and the rest payable in 4 years, with a rate of interest of 8 %. Soon after they started parcelling out the estate and selling plots to Indian small holders. Ahmode had received credit from Pipon Adam & Co and Esmael Peermamode & Co but often found himself in a difficult financial position. He had to sell his share of the estate to Abdoula in 1896 to pay his debts but bought it back three years later. He had to sell what remained of the estate again the following year and eventually died in 1920 quite penniless.

Abdoula followed him in dealing in speculative land transactions and parceling. He borrowed large sums of money from creditors in Port Louis, namely Lousteau Lalanne, W. Heerah, The Oriental Bank, A.Timol and E.Peermamode & Co. and bought estates and large plots of land, mainly in Savanne, where he lived, but also in Grand Port and Black River. He sold small plots to Indians as from 1890 but at times had to get rid of large portions of land when his credit repayments were due. Between 1889 and 1890 he had acquired various plantations of medium size, totaling 270 Arpent in surface area. Between 1896 and 1923 several large estates were acquired, namely Bois Sec, Frederica, Joli Bois, Choisy, and La Martinière as well as many medium to large portions of land from Franco-Mauritian, Gujarati, Tamil and other Indian sellers. During the same period he sold out large and small portions, for instance in 1900 he sold out 54 plots of which 37 were between 26 Perches and 2 Arpents in area, for sums varying between 50 and 600 Rupees. In that year Joli Bois was put under seizure by Brouard and Boullé who had sold the property to him on credit. In 1903 several more plots were seized by N.Jeewonjee from Port Louis, while what remained of Mont Fertile was seized by I.M.Sulliman, the Gujarati company. Meanwhile he sold large plots of land to Indian as well as Franco-Mauritian buyers like Union Bel Air. In 1922 L.Koenig put under seizure an estate of 846 Arpents situated at Savanne for default of payment and Abdoula sold large estates to F.G.Audibert, P.Ramtohul and de Sornay. He went on selling small plots of land till the 1930s and in 1931 made a last major land acquisition, jointly with his son, both then living in Vacoas, of several plots totaling 556 Arpents, from Bel Air Ltd at Chamouny.

Abdoula Dastagheer had thus dealt with a large amount of movable and immovable property at a time when few descendants of Indian indentured immigrants had emerged into large land-ownership. He seemed to have had many contacts in the financial sectors of Port Louis and enjoyed a good credit-worthiness as large sums of money were entrusted to him. Financiers were interested in investing in the parcelling out of land and used him as an intermediary, because of his relationship with the labouring class, in order to earn a profit. His inexperience, and presumably his lack of education made of him an unwise businessmen.

A Calcuttya Muslim Immigrant

Trading and other Activities

Many Calcuttya Muslim families owe their socio-economic promotion to activities in the service sector. Trade has been instrumental in the rapid capital accumulation of some families. Other ex-indentured labourers who could not invest in a plot of land or trading articles chose to operate in areas supporting agriculture, such as in transport. Others entered into a variety of manual professions. Few would rise quickly on the socio-economic scale from these occupations but the following generation could hope to move to other sectors and improve their socio-economic status.

The father of I.R was a carter in the south of the island and cultivated some crops on a rented plot. At the age of 20 I.R moved to Port Louis to help his uncle who had opened a small retail outlet for groceries. As the trade prospered he opened an outlet for himself and later moved into wholesale activities and even imported some products. He thus experienced rapid socio-economic promotion.

Trading in food and other articles often constituted the first stage in the socio-economic improvement for Bihari Muslim labourers, who then could buy some land with the savings. This movement from trade to land-ownership and cultivation and eventually back to trade was not uncommon. Bihari Muslims engaged in commercial activities at various levels, such as peddling, retail shops, wholesale shops, markets and fairs. The strong presence of Gujarati Muslims in the trading occupation may have provided an impetus to penetrate this sector. The difficulty of finding employment in a much segmented and ethnicised labour market continues to induce many Muslims into trade at various levels. Street trade and stallholding at temporary fairs has gained in importance. The commercial sector has undergone a marked expansion since Independence and the Muslims have fully participated in it.

For others who had no opportunity to go into agriculture or trade, promotion seems to have been slower by one or two generations, except in rare cases. For instance many Bihari Muslims chose to enter technical and mechanical fields. Old immigrants set up small, family enterprises such as furniture-making or tailoring in towns and small villages. Some family concerns have eventually turned into big businesses, for instance in metal works, tailoring and the furniture industry.

The father of H.T was a labourer and he himself began his working life in the same occupation. Towards the beginning of the 1930's he took employment as a manual worker in a small metal workshop which assembled buses. He opened his own workshop in 1939, which soon developed into a full-fledged industrial concern. He innovated constantly, adopting new machines, technology and material, and by the time he died in 1974 his business had grown into a major metal works enterprise which provided for the local as well as the regional markets. Many Muslims had, in the 1950's and 1960's, entered the transport business, buying one, two or more buses, which were competing with the railways. This opened opportunities for others to service this sector either through assembly workshops or in repairs and maintenance.

Moving from the labouring sector to the service sector, preceded or followed by urbanization and from then on moving towards the education of children proved to be a common itinerary. Education has often followed urbanization as facilities were concentrated in towns and transport was not easily available in all parts of the island.

Some families were able to establish themselves in the professional sector. N.S immigrated through indenture with a couple who had adopted him as a child. His son became a butcher in town, an occupation where Muslims remain well-represented for cultural reasons. He bought a plot of land during the 1920's but stayed in town so that his sons could benefit from schooling, and he travelled daily to his plantation. Several of his sons won the Junior Scholarship and attended the exclusive Royal College during the 1930's and 1940's. They completed their secondary education and joined the Civil Service. The eldest son was employed in telecommunications and acquired some in-service training in England.

There he decided to enroll in a university for an engineering degree. He paid for his studies from his savings. His younger brothers did the same, some of them paying their own way while their father and elder brothers helped the youngest ones. This family was among the first Bihari families to count a number of professionals in its ranks. Acquiring a well-paid job in the Civil Service brought prestige to Muslim families who invested in education and higher studies.

In fact Calcuttya Muslims have largely moved out of the agricultural sector in favour of the tertiary sector, with a concentration in commerce, technical and other service occupations, where they are largely self-employed. This development has been accompanied with urbanization and migration towards larger villages and regional centres. At present, 29 % of the local Muslim population is concentrated in Port Louis, where they make up 37 % of the city's population, and 29 % live in the urbanized district of Plaines Wilhems. At present about 50 % of the Muslim workforce is self-employed or work for their family enterprise while 50 % are salaried employees. The percentage occupied in the tertiary sector, is around 60 %, while those in industrial and handicraft activities stands at 20 %, with only 20 % remaining in agriculture, as wage labourers or large and small land-owners.

It is difficult to assess the importance of the economic presence of the Gujarati Muslims in the economic emancipation of Calcuttya Muslims, especially towards the end of the 19th and early part of the 20th centuries. In the above examples their role as money-lenders has been highlighted. There is in fact, plenty of evidence that they financed commercial as well as agricultural operations in the countryside, on small and large scales. This activity has certainly benefited those who received the capital but also those who made the advances. Monetary advances and even joint operations, involved Gujarati Muslims and ex-indentured Indians, irrespective of religion. However, we can presume that contact was of importance in such transactions and that Muslims had a greater opportunity, through the agency of religion, to establish and cultivate relationships with the Gujaratis. However, informants are of mixed opinion about the effective role the Gujaratis played in the emancipation of Calcuttya Muslims. Some argue that the tendency of Gujaratis to favour family and in-group members, has in fact, retarded the progress of Calcuttyas, especially in the commercial sector.

Socio-Cultural Emancipation

In 1863 a group of Bihari Muslims undertook an important community-centred task: that of building and running a mosque in Baramia, Rose Belle. This was the first mosque built in the rural areas, at the initiative of ex-indentured labourers. The leading persons were Mungroo, no. 5 324, merchant, Yeadally, no. 151 755, merchant, Peerkhan, no. 34 284, merchant, Mooradally, no.18 723, "roulier" Abdool Hakim, merchant, and Mahmod Kurrim, merchant. Mungroo arrived in Mauritius with an early batch of indentured immigrants. In 1858 he married Mookeea who had arrived as a child with her family in 1845 from Calcutta. Mungroo was a trader and a prosperous land-owner who left 32 Arpents of land at his death, in 1882. Of these he instructed his wife to donate 2 additional Arpents to the mosque. Yeadally had arrived in 1855 from the Zillah of Arrah. Peerkhan was a Pathan who arrived in 1843 aboard the "*Adelaide*" from Calcutta, together with five other Pathans. As for Mooradally, son of Fukeerah, he arrived in 1843 aboard the "*Duchess of Argyle*" from Calcutta at the age of 23. He still worked in the plantations but as an artisan, which carried a higher status than field labourer. Like the others, he seemed to have prospered in trading activities. The absence of immigrant numbers in the cases of Abdool Hakim and Mahmod Kurrim, seem to suggest that they had arrived as fare-paying passengers.

These persons went through a curious arrangement in order to build the mosque. They contributed a sum of 100 Piastres among themselves and through a collection among the Muslims of the area. The money was handed over to Mahmod Kurrim to buy a plot of land for the purpose of building a mosque. The mosque brought its founders prestige and authority in the neighbourhood as well as honour. A socio-political organisation was set up by the collectivity of mosque-users, known as the "*Jamaat*", for the running of the mosque and could exercise stringent control over the congregation and their families. A communiqué in an issue of "*L'Islamisme*" of 1910, stated that the board governing the "*jamaat*" of this mosque had decided to exclude from the congregation any person having transgressed Islamic rules, such as shaving one's beard, taking alcoholic drinks or playing cards. The son of Mungroo played a leading role in the affairs of the mosque at that date and the board included two sirdars, as well as two persons working and living on the neighbouring plantations.

This example clearly shows that the preoccupations of the immigrants, once they had improved their situation and decided to stay on the island, was to cater for their socio-cultural and religious needs and set up the necessary equipment that would help them construct a community life. A leadership role was often taken by those who were most prosperous, literate and learned or who held a higher position on the plantation. Such initiatives brought them recognition and fame but also improved their self-respect, and gained them spiritual satisfaction.

The initiative of making official the set up of the Baramia mosque, like many others that would follow over the island, was conducted through the mediation of the Gujarati social organisation of "*The Cutchi Meiman Society*". This association who ran the "*Arab Mosque*" in Port Louis and which regrouped the wealthy Meiman merchants, held a lot of prestige among the Calcuttya Muslims. This and the other Gujarati social organisation "*The Sunni Surtee Mussalman Society*", set up in the 1890's, were used as a medium from which to operate such pious enterprises. The exact role played by the Gujarati organisations varies from case to case. They seemed to intervene only as juridical facilitators in several cases of donations by Calcuttya Muslims, while in some cases they actively contributed in the building of the mosque themselves. In the latter cases the Gujarati society tended to reserve for itself the management of the mosque. In all, eight such donations were made through the *"Cutchi Meiman Society"* between 1872 and 1884, and several others though the *"Sunni Surtee Mussalman Society"*. It is clear that many Calcuttya Muslims looked up to their more fortunate Muslim co-religionists for some sort of support in their community enterprise. The majority of the mosques/*"madrasas"* (Islamic schools) were built in the countryside by the Calcuttyas, without the mediation of the Gujaratis, however.

It remains a preoccupation for the affluent Muslims to set up community-based structures to gain respect and honour from their peers. A mosque is the most popular donation but gifts to charitable and educational institutions are also highly regarded. Alhaman S. and A.Dustagheer both gave generously to construct a mosque each and an orphanage as well, in the case of the former. Travelling to Arabia for the pilgrimage and adjoining the title of *"Hajee"* to one's name also establishes respectability.

Alhaman S donated a plot of around 15 Perches in the village where he lived in the south of the island and constructed a mosque, with a *"madrasa"*, a religious school, on it. He also built a small orphanage for indigent Muslim orphans in the 1920's. He ran these institutions single-handed. He engaged religious functionaries to lead the prayers and give instruction to the children. Arabic, Urdu and the Islamic rites were taught in the madrasa. He specially engaged foreign learned men to tutor his son in Arabic, Persian, and Urdu grammar, and the marriage of his daughter was celebrated with unusual pomp in 1910. A special train was scheduled to take his guests from Curepipe to the south and a large well-decorated tent was set up to receive 2 000 guests, who were entertained with religious sermons after the marriage (*Nikah*) ceremony. Festivities lasted throughout the night and the guests were sent back on the special train at 5.00 a.m (*L'Islamisme*, 1910). The social life of the affluent Muslims was closely connected with religion. They set standards and also worked towards the building up of a sense of community through their activities. In short, islamization closely follows a rise on the economic scale and allows one to improve one's social status.

The case of A.Dustagheer is peculiar in more than one respect. Firstly, land parcelling was not a common activity among Calcuttya Muslims, if only for lack of funds. Furthermore, he also became a pioneer in politics. The Constitution of 1885 which made provision for a Legislative Council composed of 10 elected, 9 nominated and 8 official members was adopted. Right of vote was determined by property owned and education. Few Indians met with these criteria and only 400 out of 4 000 electors were from their ranks in 1886, many belonging to the merchant class of Gujarati Muslims. Under these circumstances it is curious that A.Dustagheer chose to become a candidate for the elections of 1896 and 1901.

In 1896 there were 686 Indian electors throughout the island, including 200 in Port Louis and 797 in 1901, making up around 35 % of the electorate. This figure was far from negligible and from 1891 some Indian political agents had been employed by candidates of Franco-Mauritian origin to court Indian votes. Abdoula, being well-known among the Indians and the propertied classes alike, thought he would try his luck. He stood for elections in his native district, Savanne, and though not elected, made a good score. In 1901 he obtained 72 votes at a time when the number of Indian electors in his area was only 62. This activity certainly brought him notoriety which must have helped his business. A.Dustagheer opened the way for Indians to enter politics, or at least realize the possibilities offered by political involvement.

This brief sketch of the itinerary of the indentured Bihari Muslims and their descendants highlights their great adaptability coupled with a high mobility, whether geographical or in occupational terms. Opportunities were exploited in a creative manner so as to improve the individual's and the family's position. Economic advancement was accompanied by greater religious involvement and socio-cultural integration. Status depended on a greater knowledge and practice of religion. Religion played an important part in the development of a group consciousness among the Muslims, which has largely offset the caste and regional distinctions that formerly divided them.

A Calcuttya Muslim couple

Sources and Guide for Further Reading

Deeds of land tenure and notarial acts detailing transactions in immovable property and succession, based at the Registrar General's office, have been consulted for the preparation of this article together with ships' lists, and documents concerning immigrants' marriages, and distribution on plantations, held at the Mahatma Gandhi Institute. Interviews with members of the families concerned have yielded interesting insights and complementary information. Newspapers, especially those concerned with the local Muslim community, particularly "*L'Islamisme*", from 1906 to 1907 and from 1909 to 1910 provide pertinent information about the ideas and social practices of the times. A larger study of the Muslims of Mauritius can be found in Jahangeeer-Chojoo, A. 'La communaute Musulmane de Port Louis', PhD, Bordeaux, 1987. Kalla, A.C. 'The Gujarati Merchants in Mauritius, Journal of Mauritian Studies, 1987, is the best available published source on the trader community of the island.

Religious and Cultural Traditions of Biharis in Mauritius

Sarita Boodhoo

Most Mauritians of Bihari origin descend from the indentured labourers who arrived in such great numbers between 1834 and 1860 that they became the largest segment of the population. Today, around 60% of Mauritians can still trace their origins to this region. Biharis rapidly impregnated the Mauritian cultural landscape with a strong Bhojpuri trait. The Bihari presence is manifested through their vibrant oral traditions, their patterns of dress and jewellery, their religious practices and beliefs, their medicinal plants, dietary habits, games, pastimes and artefacts.

Religious and Popular Festivals of Bihari Hindus

For the Biharis of Hindu faith, the cycle of life is directly or indirectly connected with religion. Indeed their rites of passage such as birth, the sacred thread taking ceremony, the ceremony of tonsure, the baby's naming ceremony, marriage and funeral rites, form the backbone of their cultural identity. A common sight in Mauritius is the red *Jhandi* (flag) of Hanuman floating on a long bamboo pole in front of Sanatani Bihari This is renewed annually on Hanuman Jayanti (Hanuman Day).

Another interesting visual aspect of Bihari tradition is the Kalimai. Every village has a Kalimai. A streak of vermilion (*sindur*) sanctified the stone in a field and ensured protection to those who passed by. Once consecrated in seven earthen mounds in a row, to-day the Kalimai is usually located under a 'neem' or 'peepal' tree and is fashioned in concrete. The Bahariya Puja was at one time a popular means of propitiating the goddess, and food cooked at the site would be offered to Kalimai. To-day the goat sacrifice that was associated with this *puja* has almost been discarded. In its place, at the Durga Nawmi Puja celebration, a variety of gourd is anointed with vermilion, and cut in half by the male head of the family in a symbolical gesture of sacrifice. A popular aspect of Bihari religious life which continues is the *katha* where the priests or *pundits*, hold public discourses. Men and women turn up in their hundreds in the evening, to listen to the *katha vachak* who emphasises the prevalence of goodness. Tales from Shiv Purana, Vishnu Purana, the Bhagwatam, the Ramayana and the Mahabharata were and are still recited.

Ganga Asnan

Coming as they did from the Gangetic belt, the Biharis missed the Ganges and the various river festivals which sustained their cultural life. The Sone Mela fair associated with the great ritual bath in the Ganges and the festival of Ganga Asnan held each year in the month of Kartik (October - November) have taken on a new dimension in Mauritius. Biharis here turned to the sea beaches of the island for their Kartik bath.

Maha Shivaratri

Of all the festivals brought by the Biharis, Maha Shivaratri is the most magnificently celebrated. Maha Shivaratri has also assumed an undeniable Mauritian identity and colour. The Biharis brought the Ganges along with them in their veins and consciousness and recreated a Ganga Talao in the south, at Grand Bassin, a centrally situated crater lake in the Savanne district, symbolising the underground appearance of Ganga in Mauritius. In this way Ganga continues to nurture the souls of the Biharis as it has nourished the Hindu civilization for millennia.

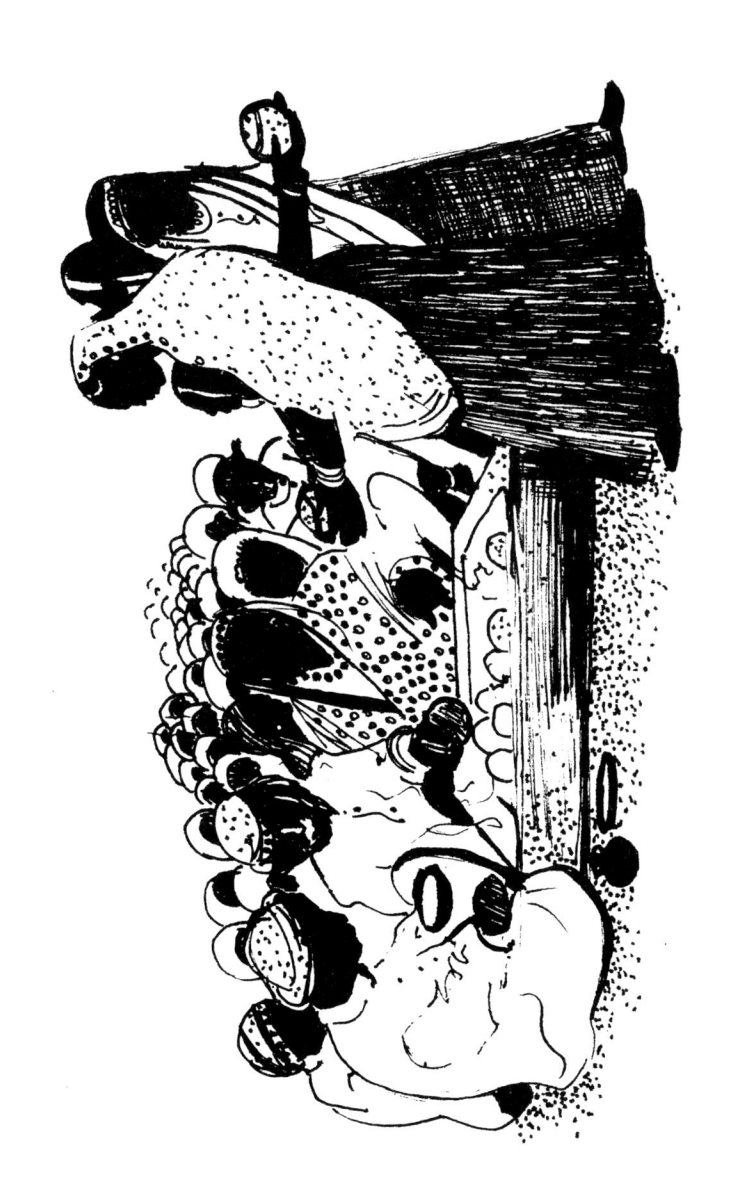

'Purnahati': A rite associated with the Durga Puja festival

Pilgrims dressed in white (a sign of purity) trek every year to the Ganga. They carry beautifully decked Kanwars, to represent a temple, on their shoulders. From the Ganga Talao, on this day in February-March, they carry back 'Ganga Jal' - Ganges water - to their respective Shivalas for the performance of *abhishekh* (the pouring of water on the Shivalingas) on the great night of Shiva.

The phenomenon of Ganga Talao in Mauritius represents a recreation of a sacred space of water to give depth and dimension to a symbol of Hindu belief. The invention of the myth that the Ganges water seeped underground to Mauritius brought to the island a Ganga beyond Ganga. Now that the Ganga flows outside India, pilgrims from Réunion Island, South Africa, U.K, France, Holland and even India come to invigorate their souls at the Ganga Talao in Mauuritius.

Dipavali

The Dipavali is the most popular Hindu festival of the island brought by the Biharis. The immigrants' huts used to be decorated with rows of earthen lamps, and today the clay lamps continue to light Biharis' homes alongside the bright displays using electric bulbs. Dipavali is asssuming a more national character in Mauritius with events organised by the Municipalities and other organisations which are enjoyed by Mauritians at large.

Ram Nawmi

Ram Nawmi, marking the birth of Rama, is also a very popular Bihari festival. The Government now grants two hours of time off work to civil servants to celebrate this joyous occasion which falls at noon, on the ninth day of the bright fortnight of the month of Chaitra (March/April).

Praying by the Sea at the Celebration of Ganga Asnan

Holi

This spring festival is also known as Phangun from the term Phalgun, the month in which it is celebrated (March/April). On the eve of the festival, Holika Dahan, the burning of the effigy of Holika, an evil woman who sought to burn her nephew, Prahlad, is celebrated, symbolic of the destruction of evil. Holi is a great celebration throughout the Bihari diaspora in Surinam, Guyana, Trinidad and Tobago, Fiji and South Africa. The celebration of Holi in Mauritius is a colourful occasion of mirth and gaiety.

Anant Vrat, celebrated on the fourteenth day of the bright fortnight (full moon period) of the Hindu month of Bhadrapad (August/September) held in honour of Lord Vishnu, is also a very popular festival among the Bhojpurias, especially the women folk, as is Karwa Chat, when young women observe *vrat* (fasts and vows) and pray for the longevity of their husbands. Biharis also share with other Hindus the Makar Sankranti, which celebrates the movement of the Sun to the tropic of Capricorn (Makar). This all-India Hindu festival is known in South India as Pongal.

Bihari Linguistic Traditions

The Biharis spoke a variety of Hindi which was known as Bhojpuri. Over the years, this language developed a standardization that imbibed a local colour and came to be known as Mauritian bhojpuri. Bhojpuri became the main vehicle of interaction and with the 'morcellements' in 1860 onwards, when Indian immigrants moved out of the barracks on the sugar estates and into their new villages, bhojpuri became the 'lingua franca' par excellence of these settlements. Even the Chinese retailer at the village corner shop communicated in bhojpuri as did the white plantation manager who dealt directly with the Indian labour force. Over time Bhojpuri speakers borrowed words from creole which they interiorised and gave a distinct bhojpuri identity. Indeed, words like 'latabwa' (table), 'lilia' (le lit - bed), 'lacouzine' (la cuisine - kitchen) are now common in Mauritian bhojpuri parlance. Similarly, bhojpuri gave many words and expressions to Creole, the expression 'caraille chaud' (the *carahi*, cooking recipient is hot) meaning things are very bad, bachara (a pejorative form of the original *bechara* (the unfortunate one), *jalsa* (amusement), *nissa* (intoxication), and *paisa* (money). Cultural expressions from bhojpuri have also percolated to Creole such as "diffé dans lanka" – literally 'there's fire in Lanka', an allusion to the Ramayana.

Bihari Folk Songs

The Bhojpuri folk songs constitute some of the richest cultural treasures of Mauritius. The folk songs from Bihar that are available in Mauritius fall into five categories: Sacraments or Sanskar geet; the Seasons or Ritu, Festivals and Fasts or Parva aur Tyohar; Work and labour or Shram geet; and other unclassified songs or Anya geet.

Of all these songs, the most popular and well-preserved are those belonging to the sacraments - the Sanskar geet. Of these, the songs associated with the various aspects of marriage rites and customs such as the time of *haldi* - applying of tumeric paste, *matikoray* – the digging of earth ceremony, and *sandhya* – the evening prayer are prevalent. The old songs brought by the immigrants are still sung at various occasions of marriage.

Each village has at least one if not several traditional women singers who attend on marriage occasions. While the priests chant the vedic hymns, the women sing in chorus about the different aspects of marriage. They sing "*jhumar*", a rhythmic song of joy, and accompany women dancing in a circle. Several other types of songs exist for each rite such as *Kanya dan* or the giving away of the daughter, *tilak* (applying the auspicious mark of respect on the bridegroom's forehead), *sindurdan, kohbar* and *bidai*, the (farewell) ceremony. Modern interpreters have reworked old songs to modern electronic music and have developed more contemporary themes. The *geet gawai* or singing session of women held on the eve of weddings honour the Goddess of light, invoking her to bless the marriage entourage so that all goes well at the time of the marriage.

Bihari Music and Dance
Entertainment at a Wedding Ceremony

Sandhya songs reflect the importance of evening prayer in the life of the Hindus. Even to this day, every evening in Bihari homes, the lady of the house will light an earthen lamp at sunset to welcome Sandhya, the Goddess of evening. In Bihar, the Sandhya songs are sung both in the morning and evening. The morning songs are no longer in existence in Mauritius.

After a round of five *sandhya* (evening), *devta* (god), *devi* (goddess), *sumiran* (invocation) and *mahadev* (in honour of Shiva) songs, the *jhumar* and melodious songs of faster rhythms and beats are sung. The women dance in circles as they sing to the tune of the *dholak* (percussion) and *lota* (a copper pitcher) beaten with two coins and spoons, an improvised instrument.

Jhumar songs reflect the influence of social customs coming from Bihar such as *dahej*, the system of dowry. These songs are no longer relevant to Mauritian Bihari society. Other songs are sung on the occasion of the *janeo* (thread giving ceremony), on the birth of a child, and on set days after the birth.

Folk songs introduced by the Biharis are also associated with the seasons such as at the time of Holi. They are sung accompanied by *dholak* and *jhal* 40 days before Holi starts on the full moon night known as Basant Panchami that heralds spring. This is known as *tal thankna* (giving the beat). They are sung exclusively by men.

In the drought period of November to February, the summer season in Mauritius, women sing the *harparawri* songs invoking Indra, the God of Rain. In 1999, when we witnessed the worst drought season in over fifty years Bihari women groups all over Mauritius sang harparawri to appeal to the God of Rain.

Work songs sung by Bihari women are known as *jatsar*. When grinding pulses and grains on the *janta* grinding stone daughters-in-law would relate their tales of woe at the hand of their mothers-in-law.

Grinding Spices

Gopal gari is a teasing and mocking satirical song intended to taunt the bridegroom's party and is not meant to be taken seriously. Such songs provide an important medium of socialisation, and no offence is meant or taken by the bridegroom's party. At the end of the singing, the bridegroom's father or his elder brother must give a token of money known as *neg* to the singing women.

There are several varieties of haldi song in existence in Mauritius. It is sung by women at the time of the application of tumeric paste on the bridegroom. As the priest and then each family member applies the tumeric paste, the women singers repeat the song naming each individual in turn:

Pehle hardiya More bipra chadhawe lan Pachey sajjan sab log	First of all the Priest applies the tumeric paste followed by the folk
Sir pe chadhaya bipra ang mein outariya ho Hirdaye se diha na ashish	Please apply the tumeric paste, Priest, on the bridegroom's head and then on all his limbs. And give blessings from the bottom of your heart.
Pehle hardiya More baba chadhawe lan Pachey sajjan sab log Sir pe chadhaya baba Ang mein outariya ho Hirdaye se diha na ashish	First of all father will apply the tumeric paste ... [repeat above stanzas]

Protest songs such as 'Moussay Manes ke mulwa' - (Mr Manes's sugar factory has been burnt down) are drawn from experiences in the sugar cane fields. Such songs as 'pani nai ba'- there is a dearth of water, symbolise a protest against the shortage of an adequate water supply. These Bhojpuri songs have been composed locally by the descendants of immigrants from Bihar on the sugar plantations. They reflect the local environment and socio-economic conditions.

Gamat or amusement songs are traditionally associated with the haldi night. Today the *gamat* is a very popular form of entertainment on the eve of the marriage and musical bands interpret traditional Bhojpuri and film songs with modern instruments. The bands have both male and women singers who are also accompanied by dance groups. Often two singers sing the *sawal – jawab* (question and answer) and compose their songs on the spot. They are accompanied by a harmonium and tabla. They sing throughout the night into the early hours of the morning. This is an old tradition in Bihar. Today in Mauritius, groups such as the Bhojpuri Boys and the Baja Baje Group, have popularised these traditional bhojpuri songs.

Rites and Rituals of Bihari Hindus

Despite the disappearance of child marriage in Mauritius, the greater interaction between engaged couples even in the case of arranged marriages, and more elaborate weddings, the rites and rituals associated with them have retained their vedic essence. The *barachia / cheinkai* ("stoppage") or betrothal ceremony is commonly known in creole as "arrete garcon, tifille ("retain" boy or girl). This is a cultural transposition of a purely Hindu tradition. The haldi rite has acquired a Mauritian colour that is unique, with a haldi dinner served after the haldi ceremony. Other wedding and post wedding rites are accompanied by customs and traditions that have a particular Bihari flavour. The *matkor* or digging of earth to build the *vedi* (wedding altar), the *domela* - meeting of bridal parties from both sides, the *parchawan* - the auspicious welcoming ceremony of the bridegroom by the bride, her mother and other married women from her side, the *Kanya Dan*, the *parikrama* - seven rounds of the sacred fire by the bride and the bridegroom, the *maroh chawai*, - auspicious construction of the wedding pavilion accompanied by women singing, and the *sindur dan* - application of vermilion on bride's mid hair parting by the bridegroom, are essentially Bihari in character. The *chauthari* post marriage ceremony held on the fourth night is a grand reception given to the bridegroom's party by the bride's parents.

Offering Water to the Tulsi Plant

Musicians accompany the bridal procession but the playing of traditional musical instruments has been replaced by taped music and the bridegroom's party no longer stay overnight at the bride's home.

At the birth of a child, the family performs *chatti* rites associated with the sixth day bath of the new mother. On this day she is shown the sun, for the first time after delivery. The sun occupies a great place in the Bihari's life. A Bihari woman usually offers water, poured over a Tulsi plant, to the sun in the morning (known as *arak dena*). The *barhi* (twelfth day ceremony) is repeated on that day after the birth. On this occasion a larger festivity is held. The new mother is now "purified" and can enter the kitchen and perform regular activities. She has also had time to rest. The *dai* or midwife was a very important figure previously. Nowadays, deliveries are performed in hospitals and clinics and the *dai* has lost her former eminence. On the 'chatti' day the *phouphou*, or baby's paternal aunt, strikes a brass *thali* (plate) with a spoon to announce the good news. The *phouphou* plays a significant role in the *mundan sanskar* when the baby's first hair is removed which she collects and immerses in a river, stream or sea. She receives a *neg*, gift for her work, as does the *dai*. The new mother is given gifts and songs known as sohars are sung to announce the good news.

Other rites of passage such as *jatta-karma* (cutting of hair ceremony), *janeo* (wearing of the sacred thread ceremony), and *namkarran sanskar*, giving of name ceremony, are also popular. The *antyesthi 'kriya'*, or funeral rites are performed according to traditional Hindu *sanskars* as in Bihar. But in Mauritius bodies are kept longer than in India to enable the relatives to attend. Ramayana singing and verses from the Gita are read before the body is taken for cremation. Cremation rites are performed either according to Puranic Brahmanic traditions or Vedic rites where a simpler prayer is said. In some cases the funeral procession to the cremation ground is accompanied by the singing of verses from Kabir's songs known as Shabad on *jhals* and *dholak*.

Weekly Ramayana singing formerly carried out by men in the baithka has now become very popular and there are Ramayana *mandalis* (associations) all over the island where men and women recite the verses of the Ram Charit Manas (Ramayana). The Ramayana singing on *jhal* and *dholak* is typical of the Bhojpuri people.

Culinary Traditions

Of all the food items introduced by the people from Bihar, it is the *dalpuri*, (Indian bread stuffed with paste of pulses) which is the most popular. This bhojpuri food prepared on the occasion of the *chawthari*, the fourth day of the marriage in honour of the bridegroom, is today one of the most popular fast foods served at most street corners in the capital, Port Louis, as well as in major towns of the island. They are also served as "take aways".

Dhal, chutneys, karhi barhi, khir, and *khichiri* are all very popular in Mauritius. The *bhindi* (lady's finger) or 'lalo' vegetable in creole is prepared in the same way as in Bihar. Bihari sweets such as *jalebi, boondiya, gawthia, laddoo* and *halwa* are all eaten. Other sweets are prepared to be offered as *prasad*. The *aloo* (potato), *kathal konkra* (pumpkin), and *chowlai* (green leaf vegetables) are prepared in the traditional way. *Namkins* or savoury cakes such as *samousas* and *bhajjias* have also been introduced by the Biharis.

Jewellery and Adornments

The *Solah shringars*, or sixteen modes of embellishment, are very popular among Bihari women, and are known as the *sorho singhar* in Bhojpuri. Bihari women normally wear their *pallu* end of the sari in front, which is known as the *anchra*. Nowadays modern Bihari women and young girls wear their pallu thrown over the left shoulder and left hanging. Women from Bihar traditionally wore *odni*, a piece of loose veil thrown over the right shoulder and which used to cover the head and the breasts. This was worn over a *jhulla*, or loose heavy blouse, or bodice and a *lahenga*, long skirt. Bihari men only wear the traditional *dhoti*, and head dress known as *pagri*, on rare occasions as at weddings and ceremonies. *Sindur*, vermilion applied on the day of the wedding in the bride's mid hair parting by the bridegroom, forms part of her daily make up thereafter.

The Bihari woman's jewellery consists of the *sikri*, the *karnphul*, the *jhumka* (earrings), the *mohar mala* or necklace, and the *peijjan* or *nupur* worn as anklets. Many of these traditional items of jewellery have become popular again in a variety of styles. The *phuli* nose ring and the *mangtikas*, - jewellery worn over the mid hair parting, are once again popular. Kajjal kohl, and *tikuli* remain in constant use. The *tika* (red dot on the forehead) remains the sign par excellence of a married woman. The *mahawar* or red paste diluted in water and applied on the bride's and bridegroom's hands and feet at the time of the wedding is also a form of decorative art introduced from Bihar.

There is today a growing desire among the people of Bihari origin in Mauritius to revive and preserve their religious and cultural traditions. Since the arrival of Biharis some of their traditions have survived in their original context while others have undergone certain transformations to adapt to the local environment. Modernity has placed its stamp on these age-old traditions. There is increasingly a reawakening of interest among younger Mauritians in these traditions and an urge to celebrate them with a new vigour and fervour.

Sketch of a Bihari Hindu woman showing traditional jewellery as worn by female immigrants in the 19th century

Sources and Guide for Further Reading

The *Bihar Gazeteer* and the *Linguistic Survey of India* by George Grierson have been consulted to provide background information about Bihar. K. Hazareesingh's *Indian Immigration*, 1975, remains a useful guide to the history of the community in Mauritius. For further information about bhojpuri rituals and traditions, see S. Boodhoo, *Kanya Dan, the whys of Hindu marriage rituals*, 1993, and *Bhojpuri Traditions in Mauritius*, 1999.

Conclusion

The articles included in this volume have sought to bring to life the patterns of settlement and processes of adaptation of Biharis in Mauritius. Through an analysis of the little known Indian immigration streams of slave and convict labour, a neglected aspect of Bihari history in Mauritius has been highlighted.

The extensive documentation available from the indenture period has been used to recreate a sense of the motivations and experiences of the men, women and children who made that fateful voyage across the kalapani. The circumstances of their roots and uprooting and the delicate process of transplantation in the new setting are described in detail.

Across the Kalapani also depicts the blossoming of Bihari traditions in Mauritius and in particular the continuities and transformations in identity and cultural manifestations which have ensued. Finally, this volume provides a survey of the enduring legacy of Bihar in the Indian Ocean - the festivals, foods, language and song which are today so much a part of the nation that is Mauritius.

Note on Contributors

Clare Anderson is Lecturer in Economic & Social History at the University of Leicester, UK. She spent a year in the Mauritian Archives, 1995-6, and has published a number of chapters and articles on Indian convict transportation. Her *Convicts In The Indian Ocean: transportation from South Asia to Mauritius, 1815-1853*, is published by Macmillan in February 2000.

Sarita Boodhoo is an advisor to the Ministry of Education in Mauritius and directs the Mauritius Bhojpuri Institute. She is a member of numerous world-wide organisations connected with the Indian and Bhojpuri Diasporas.

Marina Carter holds a doctorate in history from the University of Oxford. She is a freelance historian.

Saloni Deerpalsingh is the Curator of the Folk Museum at the Mahatma Gandhi Institute and co-author of the 3 volume *Select Documents in Indian Immigration*.

V. Govinden studied at Madras University and is a Lecturer at the Mahatma Gandhi Institute in Mauritius.

Amenah Jahangeer-Chojoo has studied at Louvain and Bordeaux and holds a PhD in Geography. She is a Lecturer at the Mahatma Gandhi Institute in Mauritius.

Note on Illustrations

The illustrations which feature in this book were commissioned from the well known Mauritian artist, **Neermala Luckeenarain**. Her pencil and pen and ink drawings capture the spontaneous charm and colour of the Bihari festivities and also vividly recreate the pain of exile and the drudgery of labour in the slave, convict and indenture periods of Mauritian history.

Note on Poetic Texts

The poems used derive from the following sources:

David Dabydeen:	*India in the Caribbean*, ed D. Dabydeen & B. Samaroo, London 1987.
Rabindranath Tagore:	*Ebar Phirao More*, translated by Rati Bartholomew and featured in Patnaik & Dingwaney, *Chains of Servitude*, New Delhi, 1985.
Khal Torabully:	kindly allowed the use of unpublished poems as well as extracts from his works, *Cale d'Etoiles, Coolitude*, La Reunion, 1992 and *Chair corail, fragments coolies*, France, 1999.
Abhimanyu Unnuth:	kindly allowed the use of his unpublished poems 'The Unknown Immigrant' and 'Kalapani'

Définissez moi je vous prie:
qu'est-ce qu'un coolie?
Celui qu'on lie au cou
pour écouler sa longue vie?

Khal Torabully